PIVOTAL
MOMENTS
IN HISTORY

THE CONQUESTS OF
GENGHIS KHAN

ALISON BEHNKE

TWENTY-FIRST CENTURY BOOKS
MINNEAPOLIS

Consultant: John Delury, Visiting Assistant Professor, Department of History, Brown University, Providence, Rhode Island

Primary source material in this text is printed over an antique-paper texture.

The image on the jacket and cover is a Persian illustration of Genghis Khan, preceeded in battle by his general, Jebe, during the invasion of the Khwarazam Empire. It is estimated to have been created in the fourteenth century.

Twenty-First Century Books
A division of Lerner Publishing Group, Inc.
241 First Avenue North
Minneapolis, MN 55401 U.S.A.

Website address: www.lernerbooks.com

Library of Congress Cataloging-in-Publication Data

Behnke, Alison.
    The conquests of Genghis Khan / by Alison Behnke.
        p.   cm. — (Pivotal moments in history)
    Includes bibliographical references and index.
    ISBN 978-0-8225-7519-1 (lib. bdg. : alk. paper)
    1. Mongols—History—To 1500—Juvenile literature 2. Genghis Khan,
1162-1227—Juvenile literature. I. Title.
    DS19.B44 2008
    950'.21—dc22   2007034073

Manufactured in the United States of America
1 2 3 4 5 6 – DP – 13 12 11 10 09 08

CONTENTS

CHAPTER ONE
LIFE AMONG THE MONGOLS

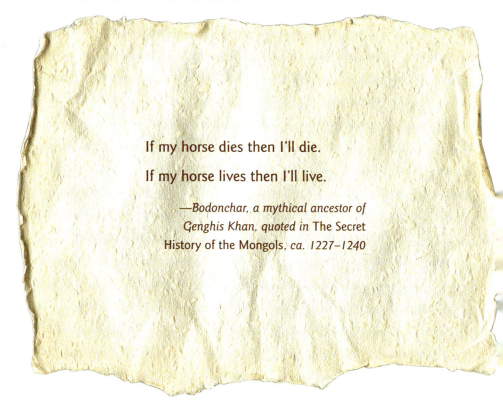

If my horse dies then I'll die.

If my horse lives then I'll live.

—Bodonchar, a mythical ancestor of
Genghis Khan, quoted in The Secret
History of the Mongols, ca. 1227–1240

The stillness of early morning was suddenly shattered by the thundering beat of horses' hooves. Enemy raiders descended on the Mongol camp, sending its frightened people running for cover. One teenaged Mongol leaped onto his horse and galloped into the wilderness. He took cover on the slopes of a nearby mountain called Burkhan Khaldun. When the danger was over, the fugitive crept back to his camp, grateful for his survival. He gave thanks to the mountain that had sheltered him, proclaiming Burkhan Khaldun to be his heavenly protector and a sacred site. He declared, "The mountain has saved my life and my horse. . . . Though I was frightened and ran like an insect, I was shielded by Mount Burkhan Khaldun. Every morning I'll offer a sacrifice to Mount Burkhan. Every day I'll pray to the mountain. Let my children and my children's children remember this."

And people would remember. For that teenager was the future Genghis Khan—the most powerful leader his Mongol people would ever know. Born as Temujin, he began life as a member of a small clan in eastern Asia and grew up in humble and difficult surroundings. But as khan, he exploded onto the world stage in the late A.D. 1100s and early 1200s. He became a great conqueror, forming the largest empire the world had yet seen—larger than that of Alexander the Great or of the ancient Roman Empire's massive realm.

His impact on the world around him was enormous, and that impact still echoes in modern times. The Mongol conquests stirred fear in the hearts of Asians and Europeans. They affected Christians, Buddhists, and Muslims. Some historians believe that this period ignited mistrust among these groups that continues to this day. Simmering tensions and rivalries continue to cause violence in the wider Middle East. Such unrest may have some of its roots in the acts of Genghis Khan and his armies.

But Genghis Khan's influence on the world around him was not strictly negative. In many ways, he proved himself a talented leader, as well as a very skillful military commander. He put into place a set of laws that guided millions of subjects. He united a vast array of peoples from different backgrounds

This sixteenth-century Persian illustration shows Genghis Khan leaning on his saddle while his horse grazes nearby.

and of different faiths and lifestyles. In ruling over his empire, he exhibited unusual tolerance of such differences for his era, yet his forces killed millions of people. He was admired by his followers and hated by his enemies. But it was precisely this combination of violence and vision—of ferocity and audacity—that made him one of the globe's great conquerors.

SETTING THE SCENE

The future Genghis Khan was born in 1162 and raised on the high Mongolian plateau, located in east central Asia. In modern times, this land is part of the nation of Mongolia, north of China and south of Russia. The area has an elevation of about 3,900 feet to almost 6,000 feet (1,189 to 1,829 meters) above sea level. Flat, mostly treeless grassland called steppes covers much of this high tableland. Rivers flow across the plains, creating some particularly fertile areas, and hills and mountains scattered around the plateau rise into the great blue Mongolian sky.

Several formidable landmasses and natural borders hem in Mongolia's steppes. Although the eastern edges are relatively open, to the west lie the Altai and Tianshan mountain ranges. South of the steppes lies the vast Gobi Desert. It covers more than 500,000 square miles (1.3 million sq. kilometers) in southern Mongolia and northern China. Part of an inland sea in prehistoric times, the modern Gobi is one of the driest places on the planet. In some years, it receives no rain at all. The Gobi is known as a "cold" desert, because winter temperatures can drop as low as –40°F (–40°C). That is not to say that the Gobi is not hot, however—high temperatures can soar to 100°F (38°C) and sometimes considerably higher. In many parts of the desert, rocky plains extend to the horizon in every direction. But the desert also has a harsh beauty and a natural magnificence that have awed people from the early Mongols to modern-day visitors.

UNCHARTED LANDS

In Genghis Khan's day, no European travelers or explorers had ever set foot in the Gobi Desert. None would until the mid-1200s, when the Italian explorer Marco Polo arrived.

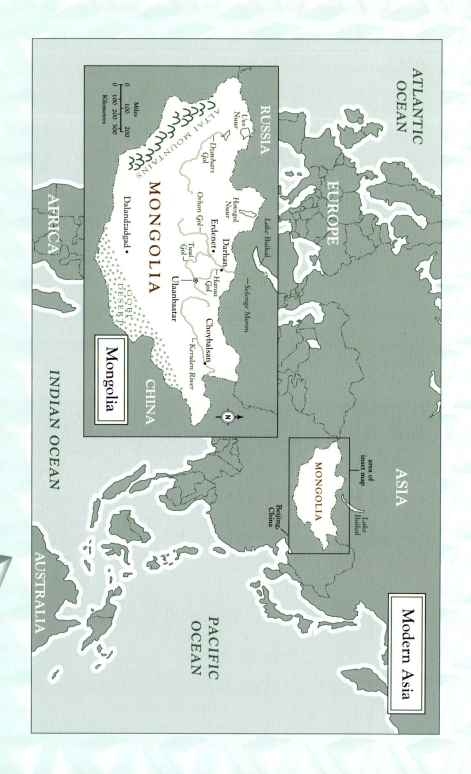

ATLANTIC
OCEAN

EUROPE

AFRICA

RUSSIA

ALTAI MOUNTAINS

Uvs
Nuur

Dzavhars
Gol

Hovsgol
Nuur

MONGOLIA

Orhon Gol

Erdenet

Darhan

Tuul
Gol

Ulaanbaatar

Harva
Gol

Lake Baikal

Selenge Moron

Choybalsan

Kerulen River

GOBI
DESERT

Dalandzadgad

CHINA

Mongolia

Miles
0   100   200   300
0 100 200 300
Kilometers

N

area of
inset map

MONGOLIA

Beijing,
China

Lake
Baikal

ASIA

INDIAN OCEAN

PACIFIC
OCEAN

AUSTRALIA

Modern Asia

Siberia makes a similarly daunting borderland to the north of Mongolia. Its dense forests and long winters make traveling through the region difficult.

In the time of Genghis Khan, these features of the landscape offered Mongolia natural defenses against enemies and invaders. They also presented challenges to the region's inhabitants, however. Freezing winds rushed down from the north in winter, bringing icy Siberian temperatures. Equally harsh at times were dry desert winds sweeping up from the Gobi. These gusts also sometimes brought dramatic thunderstorms to the region. Throughout the year, the plateau experienced dramatic temperature differences that could be as much as 140°F (79°C).

In the mid-1100s, the Mongols controlled parts of the eastern Mongolian plateau. They were not the only group in the region, however. In fact, in the early and middle twelfth century, Mongol numbers were relatively few and they were a fairly weak faction compared to other groups in the area. Other regional ethnic groups and communities—often called tribes— included the Tatars, Uighurs, Kirghiz, Naimans, Keraits, and Merkits. The exact divisions and relationships among these different groups remain unclear. Most historians believe that the

This ninth-century wall painting depicts two Uighur princes. It comes from Bezeklik, a group of artificial caves in China.

majority of the tribes shared a broad background of Mongol, Turkic, or blended Turko-Mongol ethnicity and language. Very few records on the subject exist from the period, however, so more detailed or precise information is unavailable to modern scholars.

CREATURE COMFORTS

Among the Mongols themselves were many subgroups. Some of them lived in at least semipermanent settlements. These peoples lived largely in the northern Mongolia plateau, which was more forested than the central steppes. They fished in streams and rivers, hunted the forest's wild creatures, and also raised some domesticated animals such as cattle.

Other Mongols led nomadic lifestyles. They moved from place to place across the Mongolian steppes, herding a variety of livestock. Genghis Khan would be raised in this tradition. For these Mongols, the central focus of daily life was their animals. It was these creatures that largely determined the nomadic movements of the group. In general, during times of calm, a Mongol community moved only a few times each year. These migrations took them between summer and winter pastures, always seeking good grazing land for the group's precious livestock herds.

Most of these herds were made up of sheep. These woolly animals were essential to Mongol life. Families dined on lamb and mutton (meat from adult sheep). They also drank sheep milk and made it into cheese and butter. Mongols pressed the animals' thick wool into durable felt cloth. Sheepskins became rugs and warm clothing, while leather was made into armor, saddles, and sacks. And sheep bone was shaped into arrow tips and other items.

Mongol groups also herded smaller flocks of goats. Like sheep, they provided their herders with milk, as well as meat. They also could be shorn for their wool.

Herds of horses were also essential to life in Mongolia. In fact, these animals were even more vital to a Mongol group's strength and well-being than sheep. Mongolian horses (sometimes called ponies) were small but tough. Their strong hooves did not need metal horseshoes, and the animals stayed hardy in the steppes' sometimes harsh climate. In the depths of Mongolian winter, they even knew how to dig beneath the snows to find buried grasses.

Horses were the heart of Mongol life, as they allowed Mongols to move quickly across the steppes and to cover

HISTORIC HORSES

It is almost impossible to exaggerate how important horses are in Mongol life, culture, and warfare. And they have held this exalted position for many centuries. In Asia the animals were first domesticated sometime around 4000 B.C. By 1000 B.C.— still more than two thousand years before Genghis Khan's time—the horse was already a central part of Mongol culture. Since then the genetic makeup of the sturdy Mongolian horse has changed very little. The horses that people in modern Mongolia ride, race, and breed probably look almost the same as those who served Genghis Khan and his troops.

great distances. They eased communication, trade, and war. Every young Mongol learned to ride and ride well. In addition to being strong and reliable mounts, a family's horses sometimes became food, as well. And the animals were also the source of another important traditional part of the Mongol diet—fermented mare's milk called *airag* or koumiss. Made in leather bags, this beverage contained valuable protein and calcium. It also had a slight alcohol content.

Mongol herders also kept oxen as pack animals, used especially to haul supplies when a group was on the move. Some groups also kept small herds of camels. Like oxen, these creatures served mostly as pack animals.

HEARTH AND HOME

As nomads the Mongols could pack up and be on the move on short notice when necessary. The Mongol home, called a *ger* or yurt, reflected this lifestyle. This round, tentlike dwelling had a wooden frame. The outer walls were made of a latticelike structure, held together with twine made from animal hair. Slender poles, often made of willow, formed a cone-shaped roof on top of the lattice. Heavy felt cloth made from sheep's wool covered the frame, offering protection from Siberian gusts and desert winds. Felt cloth, along with animal skins and rugs, covered the floor. A felt flap also hung in the single doorway, which always faced south or southeast. This tradition was in place largely because the winds usually blew from a northern direction. Mongols also associated the south with the sun.

Inside, gers were quite spacious, and those of wealthy families could be very large indeed. Beds and chests holding

The design of this modern ger, with its felt-covered lattice walls, is almost identical to those of Genghis's time.

clothing, food, saddles, and various household items and tools lined the outer wall of the tent, while the center was largely left open for sitting, dining, and visiting. A hole in the middle of the roof let out smoke from the central brazier (a small stove), which usually burned dried animal dung. This fire kept the ger warm and was also used for cooking.

When a Mongol group set up camp, they arranged their gers in a village called an *ordu*. The homes usually stood in a circular arrangement, with an opening to the south, and with the group's wagons and animals surrounding the tents.

Gers were quick and easy to erect and disassemble, taking as little as thirty minutes to one hour. The lattice walls folded easily, while the roof's poles were gathered up in a bundle. Once taken apart, they could be easily moved from place to place on large carts, usually pulled by teams of oxen or other livestock.

THE DAILY GRIND

In addition to the meat of their herd animals, Mongol nomads hunted and ate game animals such as antelope, wild boars, foxes, rabbits, and wolves. They usually cooked their meat by boiling or roasting it. Sometimes, however, difficult circumstances did not allow such luxuries. In these cases, riders often placed raw meat under their saddles and rode on top of it for some time to make it more tender and easier to eat without cooking. When meat was more plentiful, the surplus was placed in leather bags. Other meat was air-dried or, in winter, sometimes frozen for later use.

Animal products were not the only items on the Mongolian menu. Most Mongols supplemented their diets with millet, a cereal grain. They did not raise millet or other crops themselves but obtained it through trade with settled communities of non-nomadic groups. Mongol cooks prepared millet by boiling it. Some Mongol groups also made a sweet wine out of millet, other grains, and honey.

Tea was another popular beverage. Most Mongols obtained tea, like millet, though trade. They brewed the tea leaves in hot water, then added milk and occasionally salt to the drink.

To stay comfortable throughout the year in their changeable climate, Mongols dressed in layered clothing. Men and women alike wore a long, high-collared garment called a *del*. A wide sashlike belt was wrapped around the waist, which not only held the del in place but also offered back support during long journeys on horseback. Summer dels were generally made of light woolen felt, while those worn in wintertime were of heavier wool and sometimes had sheepskin linings.

Under the del, Mongol men wore loose-fitting pants and

women wore skirts. On their feet, they wore heavy, thick-soled leather boots, along with warm woolen socks in the winter. Mongols also wore a variety of hats and headdresses. Some were extremely practical, such as fur hats that kept riders warm in winter. Others—especially women's—were quite decorative.

Keeping a Mongol camp running smoothly meant that every person had duties and responsibilities. Women milked the livestock, made cheese from that milk, cooked the family's meals, and tended to the home's hearth. They also made woolen felt and sewed clothing. And when it was time to move camp, they were in charge of taking down the family's ger and often drove the oxen that pulled the carts. Girls grew up instructed in these skills by their mothers. Boys, meanwhile, learned to hunt and fight from their fathers. Their main jobs included watching for raiders, keeping tabs on the livestock, and retrieving animals that strayed from the herds. And all Mongol children, regardless of gender, began learning to ride horses at a young age.

FAMILY TIES

Mongol society and life were organized according to family-like groups who lived, traveled, and kept their flocks together. Subgroups or tribes within the larger Mongol ethnicity included the Borjigin and Taijut. Within these tribes were smaller entities called clans, or *omuk*. And below the clan level were still smaller subgroups known as *yasun*.

Each Mongol group had its own male chieftain, a leader who was known as a khan. His realm was sometimes called a khanate. Some of a chieftain's main duties were settling arguments among members of his clan, leading his warriors into battle when necessary, and guaranteeing the safety of the ordu and herds.

Nearly all Mongol khans came from noble families. Noble birth did not guarantee power or the right to rule, however. Tradition held that a Mongol leader remained in his position only so long as he fulfilled his duties well and commanded his people's respect. If and when he failed to live up to these expectations, his followers had the right to replace him or to find a new chieftain.

These groups and their leaders were not based solely on actual blood ties. Familial relationships often formed the basis of a clan, but so did voluntary alliances. One type of such a partnership was the *anda*, a "sworn brotherhood," or oath of blood brotherhood. Those who chose one another as blood brothers forged a strong and lasting bond. The devotion between two people who had taken the anda oath was often even greater than the connection between birth brothers.

Mongols could also choose to follow a leader who was not of their own bloodline or family. When a man chose to become a *nokhor*, or loyal follower, of an unrelated khan, he had to give up ties to his own biological ancestors. But he did so in hopes of gaining greater security and a better life for himself and his children.

FAMILY TREE

Genghis and his family came from the Borjigin tribe and the Kiyad clan.

These voluntary unions depended on trust and steadfastness to succeed. As a result, treachery and disloyalty were serious crimes and were very harshly punished—often with death.

Another link between clans and families came through intermarriage. Mongol men married women who were outside of their own clans. A wedding could bring different groups together, sometimes even creating new and beneficial bonds between former enemies. But it could also spark conflict. Women frequently became objects of competition and rivalry.

Some men—especially the wealthiest and most powerful in a group—had multiple wives. In general, one of these women was the principal, or most important, wife. She and her children had higher status in the family than her husband's other wives and their children.

In some situations, Mongol men treated their wives as property. For example, a chieftain might offer one of his wives to another leader as a token of friendship, trust, or gratitude. But in other ways, women were quite well respected in Mongol culture. Even the most powerful chiefs usually turned to their wives and mothers for advice and counsel. And some women rode alongside their husbands in battle.

SPIRITUAL LIFE

Mongols did not attend a house of worship or conduct many formal religious ceremonies. But religion and spirituality were a part of their life and culture. Genghis Khan and his fellow Mongols followed a belief system called animism. Animists believe in groups of deities (gods and goddesses) and spirits who often represent parts of the natural world.

These spirits also sometimes inhabit individual aspects of nature, such as rivers or rocks.

The most powerful figure in Mongolian spirituality was Tenger Etseg (often simply called Tenger), or Blue Heaven. This god ruled the vast Mongolian skies. Mountains and their peaks—the places closest to Tenger and his sky realm—had special importance to the Mongols. People sometimes climbed to mountaintops to offer prayers for good fortune and guidance. When doing so, they showed their respect to the god by kneeling, removing their hats, and placing their belts over their shoulders or necks. Streams and rivers were also connected with Tenger and were regarded as especially sacred.

Below Tenger's top rank was an earth and fertility goddess, Gazar Eej (also sometimes called Itugen). Mongols also revered the sun, especially the rising sun, and often knelt toward the south to pay their respects. Earth itself was also populated with a multitude of spirits. Average people were not able to communicate with these beings, however. For guidance, they turned to shamans. The shaman was a religious figure who acted as a link between humans and the spirit world. Shamans were well-respected and often very influential members of their communities. They usually dressed in white robes and rode white horses.

Among shamans' duties and abilities were offering special prayers for individuals or for the group and blessing the group's animal herds, warriors, or hunters. Shamans generally conducted ceremonies during major family events, such as the birth of a child or the death of a family member. They also sometimes carried out exorcisms of evil spirits, expelling these dangerous influences from humans. One of their most valued skills, however, was foretelling the future. The primary method of doing so was by burning the shoulder bone of a sheep and interpreting the cracks and marks that the fire left on the bone. The beating of drums helped shamans enter trancelike states, in which they communicated with spirits.

Over time, Mongols came into contact with different religions, such as Tibetan Buddhism (originating in India) and Nestorianism (a branch of Christianity that began in the Middle East and spread to China). While most Mongols did not abandon their own faith entirely, they were also receptive to the ideas of other religions. Some scholars suggest that the Mongols—who were largely a practical-minded people—thought it best to play it safe, in a sense, by not completely rejecting any possible higher powers. Nevertheless, Tenger remained their primary god.

STEPPE STRIFE

Though thus far the Mongols have been characterized as generally peaceful, conflict was a natural part of the rhythm of their lives. Occasionally strife erupted between rival Mongol clans. Mongol warriors also sometimes clashed with members of other ethnic groups, such as the Tatars and the Jin (a group living in the area that is present-day China).

Old arguments could incite rivalry and a desire for revenge for years or even decades, especially when a leader's pride was at stake. But most battles erupted over competition for territory, which was divided into provinces called *aimags*. Some land was desirable for strategic or defensive reasons. But most of the time, the areas of greatest value—

JURCHEN ROOTS

The Jin dynasty's founders were members of the Jurchen ethnic group. Centuries later, these people would come to be known as the Manchus and the region they came from would be called Manchuria.

and most worth fighting over—were those that made good grazing pasture for the nomads' precious herds.

Mongols were very skilled on horseback, a quality that made them especially formidable as warriors. The nimble feet and the great strength and stamina of their steeds also gave them an advantage over their enemies. In battle they were able to strike suddenly and retreat quickly. Bows and arrows were the Mongols' most important weapons, and they were skilled at shooting while riding. Some riders also carried other weaponry, such as swords and axes. No division existed between a civilian and a soldier in Mongol culture. The Persian historian Ata-Malik Juvaini described the Mongol troops as "a peasantry in the dress of an army." He added that "in time of need, all, from small to great, from those of high rank to those of low estate, are swordsmen, archers or spearmen."

Mongol men gained practice in the art of battle by conducting large-scale and highly organized animal hunts. In this type of hunt, called a battue, a group of hunters on horseback rode in a broad line across the plain. A few riders raced ahead and back between the other hunters and the animals, reporting on the location, number, and movements of the group's prey. Gradually—often over a period of several days—the line of hunters closed in on the animals, surrounding and trapping their prey before slaying them. The battue served well as training for warfare, giving riders the ability to group together in tight and structured formations around their enemies.

In addition, Mongols' intimate knowledge of their land's terrain and hiding places allowed them to vanish back into the wilderness. This knowledge was especially valuable in conflict with settled groups who were not so accustomed to traveling extensively through the region.

NOT QUITE FROM THE HORSE'S MOUTH

When studying Genghis Khan and the history of the Mongols, it is important to understand that even primary sources reflect only a tiny segment of the population's experiences. Most average Mongols during this period could not read or write at all. In fact, most writings about Genghis Khan, his culture, and his people came from his enemies, such as the Chinese and the Persians (inhabitants of an ancient empire centered in modern-day Iran). These writers were probably biased when the subject was their conqueror. But modern historians see these works as valuable reference tools, when taken in context.

SIGNIFICANT SOURCES

One of most important primary sources about Genghis Khan for modern writers, historians, and students is *The Secret History of the Mongols*. This book was probably written in either 1228 or 1240—soon after the khan's death in 1227. It's impossible to say whether the writer knew Genghis Khan personally. But historians are quite certain that the book was based on a rich tradition of oral history. Storytellers and minstrels kept alive these spoken stories, songs, and poems, which recorded the life and achievements of the khan in the absence of widespread written language among the Mongols. *The Secret History* is believed to be one of the first written accounts of Genghis's life and Mongol history.

Not long after the book's writing, however, it disappeared for more than a century. Descendants of Genghis Khan and officials of his empire may have been keeping it private, seeing it as a personal saga of their family and not something to be shared with outsiders. Whatever the circumstances, the work reemerged in the mid-fourteenth century. At that time, Chinese scholars translated the book into their language, and at some point afterward, the original Mongolian text vanished. Much later, *The Secret History* was translated into English, as well as many other languages.

Other important sources come from Persia and describe the Mongol invasions there. They enter the story later and therefore do not offer information on Genghis's early life, but they are very useful in studying his conquests in central Asia. One such source is the *Tarikh-i Jahangushay*, or *History of the World Conqueror*, by Persian historian Ata-Malik Juvaini. Juvaini, who was born just before Genghis's death, apparently interviewed many older people who had witnessed the Mongol invasions firsthand. He finished this volume in approximately 1259. Another late thirteenth-century Persian chronicler, Minhaj al-Siraj Juzjani, witnessed parts of the Mongol conquests of Persia himself. A later work is the *Collected Chronicles* of Persian historian Rashid al-Din. Rashid was born two decades after Genghis Khan's death but seems to have used original Mongol sources—now lost—to conduct his own research. He likely used the writings of Juvaini and Juzjani, as well. With these resources, he went on to write about Genghis and the Mongol conquests.

This early fourteenth-century Persian painting of Genghis Khan's camp illustrates Rashid al-Din's Collected Chronicles.

CHAPTER TWO

STRUGGLES ON THE STEPPES

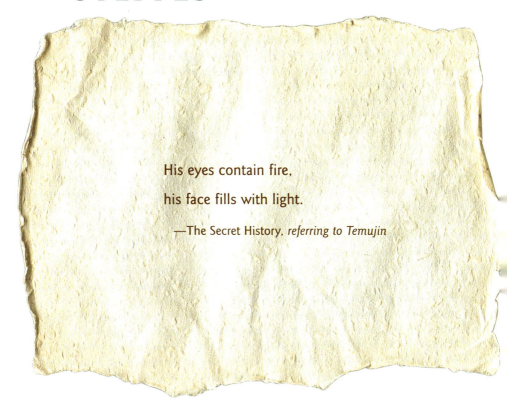

His eyes contain fire,

his face fills with light.

—The Secret History, *referring to Temujin*

In about 1162, the tents of a Mongol ordu stood in a pleasant, grassy valley. The gers lay nestled near the Onon River, which cut through the hills of the eastern Mongolian plateau. In one of these tents, a young woman gave birth to her first child. The baby's mother and father, Hoelun and Yesugei, named their newborn son Temujin, a name believed to have been that of a Tatar enemy recently defeated by the boy's father.

Young Temujin was the newest member of a long line of noble Mongols. One of his ancestors was Kabul Khan, a powerful leader who had led his clan for more than thirty years. Temujin himself was the first-born child of Mongol chieftain Yesugei Baatar, also called Yesugei the Brave or Yesugei the Valiant.

Temujin's mother, Hoelun, was a young woman from the Ongirad clan. She had become Yesugei's wife when Yesugei, with the help of his brothers, had kidnapped Hoelun from her new husband, a member of the Merkit tribe. Hoelun is said to have cried out for her former husband as she was carried off and deeply mourned being torn away from him. But she was firmly advised by her captives—and new family—to forget him. One of Yesugei's brothers chided, "This fellow who held you in his arms, he's already ridden over the mountains. This man who's lost

DATES AND DOUBTS

No one is sure exactly when Temujin was born. There is no birth certificate to consult. In fact, no records directly referring to Temujin exist from that period. Some sources from the years following Genghis Khan's death cite 1155 as his birth date, while others place his birth as late as 1167. Most sources, however, use the date 1162, and modern Mongolia uses this year for official anniversaries. That approximate date is used in this book, as well.

you, he's crossed many rivers by now. You can call out his name, but he can't see you now even if he looks back. . . . So be still now."

While the origin of Yesugei and Hoelun's marriage was hardly a story of traditional courtship, it was also not unusual for the time and place. In the Mongolian steppes, such unions were quite common. Hoelun appears to have been a strong woman who made the best of the circumstances and devoted herself to her new family.

Like other Mongol mothers, Hoelun probably wrapped her newborn son in warm sheep's wool and placed him in a wooden cradle that could be placed on her back when it was time to ride. She soon had other children to tend, as well. Temujin's family included three younger brothers and one sister who was the youngest of all. Temujin also had two half brothers, born to Yesugei's second wife. One of Temujin's closest companions as a boy was his brother Kassar, who was younger by about two years. Kassar was renowned among the clan's youths for his unusual skill with a bow and arrow.

Temujin and his siblings spent their early life in the area around the Onon River, in Khentii aimag. To the south of the Onon flowed the Kerulen, another river. These rivers provided precious water for drinking and cooking, as well as keeping the valley between them fairly green and fertile for the herds. A forested region was also close by, offering both shelter and supplies such as wood for building gers and making weapons.

Yesugei's clan of Borjigin Mongols held this desirable area. But competing clans and non-Mongol groups lived nearby and likely wanted a share of the prosperity for themselves.

A BLOODY BEGINNING

"Yesugei's people were camped at Deligun Hill on the Onon
then,
and [Hoelun] was about to give birth to her first child.
It was here that Genghis Khan was born.
As he was born
he emerged clutching a blood clot the size of a knucklebone
die in his right hand."

—from *The Secret History of the Mongols*

GROWING UP FAST

Temujin grew and learned on the great steppes. Like all
Mongol youths, he had many duties. He tended to the family's horses and other animals. He helped hunt small animals such as birds and marmots, honing his skills with bow
and arrow. He learned to ride a Mongolian horse with speed
and control.

As he grew older, he began to show a good deal of physical strength—although his brother and friend Kassar was
burlier. Temujin was also said to be quick to anger, and that
anger could be fiery.

When Temujin was around nine years old, Yesugei
decided that it was time to begin seeking a wife for his eldest
son. Riding through the steppe, they spied tents belonging
to the Ongirad people, a clan related to Hoelun by birth.
One of the tents housed a family whose young daughter was
named Borte. She was one year older than Temujin. Yesugei

took a liking to her, noticing that "she was a girl whose face filled with light, whose eyes filled with fire."

After discussing the match, both fathers gave their consent for a marriage between their children. Yesugei rode off, leaving Temujin behind with Borte and her father to begin getting to know the family. But as Yesugei traveled toward home himself, he stopped for a rest at a Tatar clan. No one is certain why he made such a choice, as the Tatars were a long-standing enemy of the Mongols and of Yesugei's Borjigins, in particular. A few days later, back at his own ordu, Yesugei fell seriously ill. As his clansmen watched him ailing in his tent, many of them believed that the chieftain had been poisoned by his Tatar foes.

Clan elders sent word to Temujin, who left Borte and rode off to his father's side. But he reached Yesugei too late. The chieftain had already died, plunging Temujin and the rest of his family into mourning. And suddenly, at only about ten years old, Temujin was abruptly thrust into the role of his clan's potential chieftain.

He would not take the position automatically, however. In the wake of Yesugei's sudden death, the clan he had commanded rapidly began to scatter. After all, what kind of leader could a boy of fewer than fifteen years be to them? Fearful for their futures, most of the clansmen and their families rode off in search of someone new to protect and lead them.

HARD DAYS

Things were bleak for Temujin and his family in the days, weeks, and years following their patriarch's passing. Not only did nearly all of their fellow clan members—even Yesugei's brothers—abandon them, but they took the herds and most other possessions of the clan along with them. Hoelun and her children were left to fend for themselves.

But the little family was tough. Mother and sons fished in the streams, using clumsily made hooks and nets. They learned to glean what little food they could from the land, including wild plants such as pears and onions. Over time they gathered a few humble possessions, along with the most valuable assets of all—a modest herd of sheep and nine horses. Together they forged a difficult and meager life, while Temujin and his brothers grew in strength, experience, and determination.

But strife sometimes erupted even within the tiny group. Temujin's pride and fierce will—and, probably, his frustration with his once-influential family's diminished way of life—brought him into conflict with Begter, the older of his two half brothers. In *The Secret History*'s version of events, Begter angered Temujin by taking a bird that Temujin had shot and later a fish that Temujin and Kassar had caught. Outraged and indignant, Temujin complained to his mother. But rather than siding with her eldest son, Hoelun scolded him for starting petty quarrels at such a dire time for the family.

"Stop this!" she commanded, according to *The Secret History*. "How can brothers act this way with each other? No, when we've no one to fight beside us but our own shadows, when there's nothing to whip our horses but their own tails . . . why do you fight among yourselves?"

Despite their mother's words, the headstrong Temujin and Kassar resolved to pay back Begter. And so they did.

A Chinese artist of the fourteenth century painted this image of a Mongol archer on horseback.

Holding their bows and arrows, they found Begter where he watched the family's horses and shot him—fatally.

Death may seem like a high penalty for the theft of a bird and a fish. Many scholars think there was more than mere revenge involved in this bloody incident. Temujin may have viewed Begter as a potential rival for the position of the family's new leader. For one thing, Begter seems to have been about the same age as Temujin—possibly even a little older. According to Mongol custom, Begter could have eventually married Hoelun and officially become the head of the family. Begter's murder eliminated Temujin's primary competitor. Clearly, Temujin already had a spark of ambition in him.

Some historians believe that the way Temujin and Kassar went about attacking Begter also revealed an early glimpse of Temujin's talent for military organization. Although Temujin was not a bad archer himself, Kassar was much more skilled. Kassar, on the other hand, does not seem to have been the brightest of boys, suggesting that his older brother planned the strike. According to *The Secret History*, Kassar approached Begter from the front, while Temujin crept up from behind. This gave the better shooter the harder task and gave Temujin more time to take his shot.

Whatever Temujin's motives, however, when Hoelun found out what her hotheaded sons had done, she was furious. She shouted at them for betraying their own family, for acting rashly, and for disobeying her first warning. But—perhaps thinking that the family had been through enough—she did not banish or abandon her sons. Interestingly, Begter's own brother, Belgutei, forgave Temujin and Kassar. In fact, he came to be a devoted friend and follower of Temujin.

Such bonds were important. For as it turned out, new challenges were in store for the family—this time from beyond their camp's borders.

THE FIRST CHALLENGE

Hoelun had been right to urge her children to keep peace with one another. The family had plenty of enemies and rivals beyond the circle of their tiny camp. For one, they would likely face challenges from Hoelun's former Merkit clansmen, who might well take advantage of the family's misfortune and isolation to pay back Yesugei's descendants for kidnapping Hoelun as a young bride.

But Temujin's first major threat did not come from the Merkits. When he was about fourteen years old, he faced a challenge from a chieftain named Targoutai Kiriltuk. This man was a former follower of Yesugei and a member of the Taijut tribe. After Yesugei's death, Kiriltuk had managed to take command of many of the dead leader's former clansmen. Historians are not sure why he next set his sights on defeating Temujin—who was, after all, still a boy. Perhaps he saw the youngster as a potential rival. Or perhaps he took it upon himself to punish Temujin for the murder of Begter. In any case, Kiriltuk and some of his men rode into Hoelun's little camp. The family fled on horseback, concealing themselves among nearby forests and caves. But after several days, hunger drove a desperate Temujin out of his hiding place—and to the waiting Taijuts. The Taijuts took their young captive back to their own camp, placing him in a *cangue*. This traditional device was made of a hinged wooden board with a hole in the center. This "collar" locked around the prisoner's neck, allowing him to walk but vastly reducing his mobility.

So shackled, Temujin remained Kiriltuk's prisoner for some time. As the Taijuts moved from camp to camp, they dragged their captive along with them. But Temujin appears to have watched closely for a chance to escape. Finally, when the camp's men were celebrating a holiday and he had only one guard, he made his move. He used the very cangue that held him to hit his guard on the head, and he ran out into the night. When he heard a search party coming for him, he lowered himself into the nearby river and hid in the tall reeds along the bank. But one man caught a glimpse of him—and said nothing. Temujin noticed and took note.

This man—whose name was Sorkhan Shira—was not from the Taijut tribe, but rather from another group that had been conquered by the Taijuts. Therefore, having relatively little loyalty to Kiriltuk and his people, he made a perfect potential ally. Indeed, he apparently felt sorry for Temujin and his predicament, for he kept silent after spotting him in the reeds. But *The Secret History* suggests that he got more than he bargained for when Temujin, cangue and all, later showed up at his ger seeking protection. Sorkhan Shira knew that to be caught with the prisoner would mean severe punishment for them both. So he agreed to help the boy, removing the cangue and burning it to destroy the evidence. Supplying Temujin with dry clothes and a bit of aimag, he sent him back to his own family. With Sorkhan Shira's help and through a mixture of his own daring and cleverness, Temujin had escaped a dangerous situation.

FRIENDS AND FOES

At some point during these important years of Temujin's youth, he met a boy named Jamuka. Jamuka was about the same age as Temujin and was a member of the Jadirat clan of the Mongols. Like Temujin himself, Jamuka was of noble birth within his people. When Jamuka's family camped near Temujin's camp, the two youths became very close friends. They went on to swear the anda oath. As blood brothers, they exchanged gifts with each other to show their devotion.

Meanwhile, enemies still lurked. Not long after Temujin's escape from the Taijuts, the family suffered a terrible setback when raiders stole eight of their nine horses—the group's most valuable possessions. Although Belgutei and Kassar both volunteered to go after the thieves, Temujin, the oldest, insisted on going himself. Riding the family's one remaining steed, he set out after the raiders, tracking their path across the steppes.

Along the way, Temujin encountered a boy a little younger than himself. He asked the youth, whose name was Borchu, if he had seen the culprits. Borchu replied that he had and offered to ride after them alongside Temujin. The pair found and reclaimed the eight stolen animals and turned back across the plains toward Temujin's camp. They managed to evade the thieves as night fell.

Grateful to the boy who had helped him, Temujin offered to give him some of the recovered horses. But Borchu refused, saying, according to *The Secret History*, "When I saw you were in trouble I said, 'I'll be your friend and I'll help you.' Should I take your horses now like they were my spoils?" From that time on, Borchu became one of Temujin's closest friends and most trusted allies.

OLD PROMISES, OLD SCORES

When Temujin was about sixteen years old—probably in about 1178—he decided the time had come to return to his chosen bride, Borte. The marriage would not only give him a partner and a mother for children of his own but would also allow him to claim Borte's family and their Ongirad clan among his own allies and potential followers.

So Temujin rode out to Borte's family's camp, where the pair were officially wed. Following what were probably great festivities, Borte accompanied Temujin back to his own camp—and now hers. With her she brought a beautiful cloak made of black sable fur. This luxurious garment was meant as a gift for Hoelun, the new bride's mother-in-law. But Temujin had an idea to turn the glossy cloak into something even grander.

Years earlier, Temujin's father had taken the anda oath with a man named Toghrul. Toghrul was a powerful chief of the Keraits, a tribe with Turkic origins. His territory was large, extending over much of the western Mongolian plateau and also southward across the Gobi. And as the son of Toghrul's dead anda brother, Temujin had the right to turn to the chief for protection and aid. For Temujin, an alliance with such a powerful leader could dramatically improve his fortunes. It would offer his family greater protection, while he himself could gain in experience, reputation, and importance.

But until now, Temujin had held off making such a request for help. He was too proud—and too savvy—to go to Toghrul as a powerless boy, with nothing to offer in return. But Borte's magnificent fur finally gave him something to present as a token of thanks and a symbol of his own dignity. With Belgutei and Kassar at his side and the sable in his hands, he met with Toghrul.

Toghrul accepted the fur and agreed to take on Temujin as a sort of adopted son. He pledged, "In return for this coat of sables I'll get back all your people who've scattered. In return for this coat of sables I'll round up all your people who've gone separate ways."

This position was probably not one of very high rank for Temujin. Toghrul most likely saw the young man as a subordinate associate, not an ally of equal status. But the agreement did offer Temujin the security that he and his family had lacked for so long.

Around the time of sealing this pact with Toghrul, Temujin also acquired a new friend and follower—a young man named Jelme. Some accounts say that the two met by chance as Temujin traveled across the steppes. Others suggest that Jelme's father sent him to Temujin, perhaps honoring some old promise to Yesugei. In any case, Jelme—like Borchu—would become a trusted companion and one of Temujin's first true followers.

Not long after Temujin made his valuable connection with Toghrul, he had the first occasion to call upon the older man to honor it. To the north, the Merkit tribe had not forgotten their rivalries with the Borjigin Mongols—including Yesugei's kidnapping of Hoelun. When Temujin was about nineteen years old, the Merkits decided to settle that old score. Very early one morning, a group of Merkits on horseback galloped into Temujin's family camp, scattering the inhabitants.

Temujin mounted one horse and fled into the wilderness. Hoelun did the same, clutching her youngest child, the girl Temulun, on her lap. Most of the family managed to escape, racing across the valley toward the nearby mountain of Burkhan Khaldun. But somehow, Borte was left behind, and a Merkit raider swept up Temujin's new wife.

The attackers then attempted to track down Temujin himself, but he was too well hidden in Burkhan Khaldun's thick forests and muddy foothills. After several days, they gave up the search. With Borte still in their possession, the Merkit raiders rode off once more. Back in their own territory, they gave Borte as a wife to a man related to Hoelun's former husband. For the moment, the score was settled.

But of course, it would not remain so. Temujin had no intention of losing Borte without a fight and wasted little time in calling upon Toghrul for his aid in rescuing his bride. He also asked his blood brother, Jamuka, for his help. Jamuka had by that time become a respected leader among his own clan and commanded hundreds of men. Both Toghrul and Jamuka agreed to help Temujin in his fight and committed warriors to the task.

The three groups of soldiers came together in a valley and with their combined forces—numbering in the thousands—attacked the large Merkit camp. Chaos erupted as

This illustration in Rashid al-Din's Collected Chronicles shows one group of Mongol warriors shooting at another Mongol group.

most of the Merkits tried to escape, loading their carts and scattering into the surrounding country. Those who could not flee fast enough became prisoners of the attacking forces. Some female captives would become wives. The attackers also raided their victims' tents, plundering them for loot.

Meanwhile, Temujin rode through the tents, shouting Borte's name. According to *The Secret History*, Borte heard her husband's voice and came running to him amidst the confusion. Embracing his wife, Temujin called out to his comrades. "I've found what I came for," he declared. "Let's go no further."

The battle had been a great success, and word of it spread through the region. Temujin had participated in his first major victory.

BEGINNINGS AND ENDINGS

Following their fight against the Merkits, Jamuka and Temujin combined their camps and clans, living and traveling together as one large group. *The Secret History* describes them saying to each other, "We've heard the elders say, 'When two men become anda their lives become one. One will never desert the other and will always defend him.' This is the way we'll act from now on. We'll renew our old pledge and love each other forever." So saying, the pair renewed their anda oaths and exchanged gifts once more. For months they were inseparable companions.

But after about one and a half years, some rift divided the friends. In *The Secret History*'s version of events, the quarrel seems to have begun over a disagreement about where the group should make camp. In any case, Temujin and Jamuka abruptly stopped traveling together and made separate camps.

Meanwhile, a happier event took place for Temujin and his family. Not long after her kidnapping by the Merkits, Borte learned that she was pregnant. The following season, she and Temujin welcomed their first child—a son named Jochi. Now in approximately his early twenties, Temujin was a husband, a new father, and the head of a small but very tough group.

THE PARENT TRAP

The timing of Borte's pregnancy left some doubt as to whether Temujin was the child's father. It was possible that the biological father was actually the Merkit man to whom Borte had been given as a wife. This uncertainty, however, did not cast a shadow over Jochi's birth. And as far as historians can tell, Temujin did not treat this son differently from his other children. In fact, the situation was not especially unusual. Because the kidnapping of women and wives was common on the steppes, many families had children who were born in similar circumstances. Mongol tradition dictated that such uncertainty should not lead a father to treat those children any differently from the others in a family.

CHAPTER THREE

Forging a Mongol Nation

And so in the Year of the Tiger,

having set in order the lives

of all the people whose tents are protected by skirts of felt,

the Mongol clans assembled at the head of the Onon.

They raised a white standard of nine tails

and proclaimed Genghis Khan the Great Khan.

—*from* The Secret History

Over the previous few years, Temujin's status on the steppes had risen considerably. His partnership with Toghrul was one factor in this advancement. His successful attack against the Merkits had also improved his reputation significantly, proving that he could—and would—fight and win a battle when necessary. Gradually, especially following his split with Jamuka, he began gaining in power and prestige. Most important of all, he began gathering a group of followers around him. Some of these people were his clansmen. For example, one of Yesugei's brothers—Temujin's uncle—came to Temujin's camp. Others, however, were from different Mongol groups but chose to join him just the same. Perhaps they were dissatisfied with their current leaders and saw in Temujin a flash of something special. Accounts seem to indicate that he was a charismatic young man, capable of inspiring respect and loyalty among others. In addition, *The Secret History* tells us that tales of omens and signs, showing that Temujin was favored by the heavens, had begun to spread across the steppes. These stories, too, may have attracted new followers.

Jamuka still commanded a larger group than Temujin. He also claimed more important figures, with many tribal chiefs and their own followers among his allies. Temujin, in contrast, oversaw a somewhat ragtag group, made up of loyal friends, small bands, and individuals who had been unhappy else-where. And he still had to be on guard at all times against possible threats to his small group and his tenuous hold on power. Nevertheless, there was no question that he had dramatically improved his situation and that of his family—especially compared to the dark and hopeless days following Yesugei's death.

A GRAND VISION

As Temujin's power and influence grew, so did his ambition for still greater glory. He had begun to have visions of a much grander goal—the unification of the Mongol tribes into a single force.

Several other groups in the region, such as the Keraits, Naimans, and Tatars, had largely achieved this kind of unity.

They were still comprised of smaller related tribes, but these subdivisions lived in relative peace with one another. The Mongols, on the other hand, were not unified in Temujin's day and had not been for many generations. Mongol subgroups often fought one another. These clashes used resources and energy. As other groups grew more unified, Mongol factions struggled to counter attacks from their larger and more powerful neighbors. As a result, Mongols were one of the weakest factions on the steppes in the late twelfth century.

BECOMING KHAN

A major first step toward Temujin's lofty intentions was officially being declared a khan. Simply having followers was not enough. He needed the legitimacy that the formal title would give him, both among his fellow Mongols and in the eyes of other groups.

In about 1190, Temujin—then nearly thirty years old—held a *kurultai* to discuss his election as khan. The kurultai was the traditional Mongol conference, and it brought together a clan or group and its most important members. Historians believe that the 1190 kurultai took place on the shores of a lake not far from Burkhan Khaldun, Temujin's sacred mountain.

Temujin was by no means guaranteed the title of khan. One complication was the fact that many of the relatives who had joined him were his elders. As such, they could technically claim a greater right than he could to the clan's supreme leadership. But he also had factors on his side. He was of noble birth. He had already enjoyed some military success. And he had an alliance with the powerful Toghrul. In addition, he had several extremely loyal followers—not to mention the apparent approval of heaven. When the kurultai was over, he emerged as his people's khan.

The Secret History cites a dramatic speech given by Temujin's older relatives as they pledged loyalty to their new khan:

> "Temujin, if you'll be our Khan
> we'll search through the spoils
> for the beautiful women . . .
> for the great palace tents . . .
> for the finest geldings [castrated male horses] and mares.
> We'll gather all these things and bring them to you.
> When we go off to hunt for wild game
> we'll go out first to drive them together for you to kill.
> We'll drive the wild animals of the steppe together
> so that their bellies are touching. . . .
> If we disobey your command during battle
> take away our possessions, our children, and wives.
> Leave us behind in the dust,
> cutting off our heads where we stand and letting
> them fall to the ground.
> If we disobey your counsel in peacetime . . .
> Leave us behind when you move,
> abandoned in the desert without a protector."
> Having given their word,
> having taken this oath,
> they proclaimed Temujin Khan of the Mongol.

BLOOD FEUD

Temujin's election as khan seemed to accelerate a separate conflict that had been brewing ever since his break with Jamuka. Both men were ambitious. But only one could be the Mongols' supreme leader. A clash between the old blood brothers seemed inevitable. In the early 1190s—approximately one year after Temujin became khan—the simmering rivalry boiled over.

Jamuka appears to have begun the clash. Sources suggest that he used a minor interclan incident over a stolen animal as a reason to go to war with Temujin. In any case, Jamuka organized a fighting force and prepared to march against his former friend. Historians don't know how many men Jamuka assembled, and estimates range from a few hundred up to twenty thousand or thirty thousand men.

Fortunately for Temujin and his band—who probably had a smaller number of fighters—they were forewarned when a pair of local men sent word to them of the approaching force. While that warning may well have saved the young khan from complete annihilation, it was far too little to guarantee his victory. When the groups met in battle, Temujin's forces simply could not hold out against Jamuka's onslaught. They soon fled in disorder, with the khan himself finding refuge once again in the foothills of the mountains—possibly even at Burkhan Khaldun—at the edge of the steppes. Once again, he was a fugitive.

Some accounts do record a side effect of Temujin's loss to his old anda that, while grim, was somewhat helpful to Temujin himself. These accounts report that Jamuka executed seventy prisoners after the battle, through the grisly method of boiling them alive. Some historians believe that some of

HEAVEN KNOWS

One of the people who joined Temujin after his defeat by Jamuka claimed to have seen a vision proclaiming the khan as a leader favored by the gods. This visionary told the Mongols of what he'd seen: "A hornless white ox appeared . . . and it came up behind Temujin, bellowing again and again: 'Heaven and Earth have agreed that Temujin shall be Lord of the Empire.'"

Jamuka's followers were so appalled by the cruelty of this punishment that they deserted him, joining Temujin instead.

TATAR INVOLVEMENT

Politics to the south soon played a role in Temujin's ongoing struggle for supremacy. Across the Gobi, the Jin dynasty (ruling family) lived and ruled in present-day northeastern China. The Jin rulers were a very powerful group, commanding a significant empire. Nevertheless, they had long struggled with the many groups living to their north. As a settled realm, with permanent cities and villages, they battled against raids and other attacks from the various nomadic tribes.

To counter such threats, Jin officials had developed a strategy that so far had served them well. Whenever one nomadic group grew strong enough to pose a real danger, Jin leaders turned to another, less powerful faction for help in checking that strength. They often offered rewards—such as the booty captured in battle—to the weaker group for their assistance. By playing the various nomadic groups against one another in this way, the Jin kept all of them relatively weak and held on to the greatest advantage themselves.

In about 1195, the group that posed the biggest threat to the Jin realm was the Tatars. The Tatars were also old enemies of the Borjigin clan—especially in the wake of Yesugei's suspicious death. So Temujin leaped at the chance to help the Jin defeat this rival group. Whether the Jin specifically asked the young khan for his help is uncertain, however—as is whether or not Toghrul took part in the campaign. In any case, Temujin and his forces took up the cause.

Jin forces attacking the Tatars from the south and east drove them northward across the steppes. In turn, Temujin's men (and possibly Toghrul's) blocked their escape routes, hemming them in. The Tatar forces were trapped. The battle that followed was relatively short, with many Tatars attempting to flee rather than fight. Temujin's men defeated them with little difficulty.

Pleased Jin officials rewarded Temujin with an honorary title that meant "pacifier," or "keeper of the frontier." Toghrul also had a Jin title, that of Ong Khan (Wang Khan, in Chinese), meaning "prince" or "king." But experts are not sure whether the Jin gave him this honor because he participated in this campaign or for some other assistance.

This victory over the Tatars was particularly important for Temujin personally, as it exacted revenge for Yesugei's death. In addition, the Tatars held a great deal of wealth—which Temujin and his fellow victors were then able to claim for themselves as the spoils of war. *The Secret History* describes a "silver cradle and a blanket covered with pearls" as among the most valuable loot.

LOST TIME

Following Temujin's defeat at Jamuka's hands in the 1190s, a gap appears in *The Secret History* and other sources. No one seems to know for sure what Temujin did for the next several years—possibly as long as a decade. One Chinese author claims that Temujin became a prisoner of the Jin people. Other sources speak vaguely of ups and downs, challenges and victories. Certainly, by the mid-1190s—and especially following the victory over the Tatars—Temujin had conquered a large number of Mongol clans and had solidified his control over much of the steppes. Whatever took place during these "missing" years, Temujin held on to the title of khan and remained a force to be reckoned with.

Defeating the Tatars also gave Temujin what he wanted and needed most of all—more men under his command. Some came directly from the victory, in the form of captives. Others arrived in a more roundabout way, attracted by the khan's new wealth and ever-increasing power. The more people who followed him, the more followers he attracted, in turn.

ONGOING STRUGGLES

By approximately the beginning of the thirteenth century, Temujin had secured power over most of the area's tribes. It had not been an easy task, nor a quick one—it had, after all, taken about a decade of fighting. Finally, however, the khan had nearly reached his goal of forging a unified

Mongol confederation. Still, though, a few major rivals and threats stood in his way. The first of these was Jamuka.

In about 1200 or 1201, Jamuka had adopted the title Gurkhan. It was an ancient name, meaning "universal ruler." By taking this powerful title, Jamuka made a direct challenge to Temujin's own authority as khan. In essence, Jamuka was declaring that he, not Temujin, would rule over all Mongols and become the greatest single leader in the steppes. In making this claim, Jamuka had support from a wide variety of tribes and clans—most of whom sided with him because they feared Temujin's strength.

Toghrul's warriors joined Temujin's, and they met Jamuka's men in battle. This time, Jamuka appears to have had the smaller force. Temujin and Toghrul drove back Jamuka's forces, and Jamuka himself fled. Temujin's men went on to beat the Taijuts, who had been part of Jamuka's coalition. Perhaps remembering his captivity among the Taijuts in his youth, Temujin showed no mercy to the defeated foe. He ordered the execution of most of the tribe's men.

In the fight against the Taijuts, an arrow struck and killed Temujin's horse. Following the battle, as captives were rounded up, one man came forward and confessed to being the archer who had fired the fatal arrow. *The Secret History* reports that Temujin was impressed with the man's honesty and bravery in owning up to the deed. He accepted him as a follower and gave him the name Jebe, meaning "arrow." Jebe would become a loyal and talented commander.

In 1202 Temujin and Toghrul joined forces against another old foe. They launched an assault on the Tatars, once again emerging victorious. This time, Temujin did not leave the Tatars to regroup. He directed his forces to kill the men and to take the women and many children as slaves. He chose two Tatar women himself as wives.

This win and its aftermath decisively broke the power of one of Temujin's strongest and oldest enemies. The Tatars were virtually annihilated as a group, and Temujin was closer than ever to ruling over all the steppes.

THE FACE-OFF

In about 1202 or 1203, Temujin's longtime ally Toghrul was growing old. He would soon be looking for a successor as ruler of the Keraits. Toghrul had a son, Senggum, but he appears to have had relatively little power and little talent as a leader. Temujin, in contrast, had transformed from a nearly powerless boy to a mighty khan. He must have appeared a worthy heir to Toghrul's throne.

Senggum seems to have envied Temujin and his close connection to Toghrul. Despite his shortcomings, Senggum likely aspired to inherit his father's position and power. Seeking to weaken the bond between Temujin and Toghrul, he urged his father not to trust the young khan.

Did Toghrul have cause to mistrust Temujin? The sources do not agree on all that had passed between the two men over the years. Toghrul may have schemed against Temujin at times or at least been less than fully supportive of his ally. And Temujin may well have aspired to take over the Kerait kingdom eventually.

But more than once, Temujin seems to have given Toghrul clear reassurances through actions. In one instance, when

Two Mongol warriors fight, one with a lance (left) and the other with sword and shield. Both carry bows and arrows. A Persian artist created this painting in the fifteenth century.

Toghrul's own brother had forced him from power, Temujin sent forces to restore Toghrul to his throne. In another case, Toghrul was fighting Naiman forces when the enemy kidnapped his wife and son. When Toghrul turned to Temujin for help, the younger khan sent four of his best war- riors to help his ally recover his family.

Nevertheless, Senggum had some success in his effort to turn his father against Temujin. He seems, for example, to have derailed Temujin's attempts to forge further bonds between the Keraits and the Mongols through marriage. Temujin proposed a match between Toghrul's daughter and Temujin's eldest son, Jochi, as well as between one of Temujin's daughters and one of Senggum's sons. Perhaps at Senggum's urging, Toghrul's family rejected the marriage proposals—a grave insult to Temujin.

Meanwhile, Senggum built alliances of his own. He found a supporter in one of Temujin's greatest foes—Jamuka. Several other high-ranking leaders also joined forces with Senggum, probably believing it was their best chance to pre- vent their absolute domination by Temujin.

Toghrul himself appears to have been deeply distressed by the choice he was forced to make. *The Secret History* quotes him as crying, "How can I betray my own son? How can we think evil of a man who's supported us in our greatest troubles?" In the end, torn between his biological son and his anda son, the elderly Toghrul simply did not have it in him to side against Senggum.

With a growing coalition in place, Senggum set a trap for Temujin. Claiming to have changed his mind about the marriage proposal, he invited the Mongol khan to come to the Kerait camp for the weddings and accompanying celebration. Pleased, Temujin set off with a small group of companions. Whether he was tipped off to Senggum's plan by a friend or a spy or simply grew suspicious is unclear. In any case, he turned back.

With his plot exposed, Senggum readied his men to begin a more direct battle. But Temujin was unprepared for such a conflict. As Temujin retreated, Senggum appears to have cornered him and forced him into battle near modern-day Manchuria. While some sources suggest that Temujin's men won the fight, that outcome is unlikely under the circumstances. Instead, it seems that Temujin retreated in disarray, many of his men taking flight across the steppe in different directions. During the fighting, his own son Ogodei was badly wounded. Finally, with only a small number of troops and a handful of his closest followers still at his side, Temujin reached the shores of the muddy Baljuna (a lake or river somewhere in southeastern Mongolia). He set up a camp there in approximately the summer of 1203.

UP FROM THE ASHES

The outlook at Baljuna was undeniably bleak. Temujin's forces had been widely scattered, and his enemies were teaming up in hopes of breaking his power completely. But he did not lose his resolve. A story passed down through the ages describes an oath sworn between himself and the leaders who accompanied him.

> Upon arrival at the Baljuna, the provisions were used up. It happened that from the north a wild horse ran up. Kasar brought it down. From its skin they made a kettle; with a stone they got fire, and from the river, water. They boiled the flesh of the horse and ate it. [Temujin], raising his hand toward the sky, swore thus: "If I finish the 'great work,' then I shall share with you men the sweet and the bitter; if I break my word, then let me be as this water." Among the officers and men, there was none who was not moved to tears.

With their loyalty thus declared, this little band passed a hard few months together at Baljuna. Temujin used the time to begin re-forming his alliances and building new ones, sending messages around the steppes. One of these communications went to Toghrul himself. Temujin appealed to the old leader to recall their alliance—to honor the oath of anda that had bound Toghrul first to Yesugei and now to Temujin. He reminded him of the many times the younger man had helped him. Temujin also contacted leaders of various tribes—including some who had defected to Toghrul and Senggum's coalition—inviting them back to his side.

Toghrul seems to have been shamed by Temujin's reproach. He apparently made no move to stop Senggum from carrying out his plans against Temujin, however. But others answered the Mongol khan's call, joining forces with him once more and swelling the ranks of his troops and followers. For example, the Ongirad people, related to Temujin's wife Borte and to his mother, Hoelun, pledged their support. So did several other Mongol clans, as well as some groups from non-Mongol tribes. During this time, Temujin probably forged ties with peoples including the Khitans and the Onguts—both of whom would be valuable allies to him later.

Meanwhile, Senggum's coalition began to disintegrate. In about 1204, the time was right for Temujin to reemerge from Baljuna and go to war against Toghrul and Senggum. He launched a surprise attack on the Kerait camp and, after three days of battle, defeated the foe. Toghrul fled from the battlefield and was killed by a Naiman soldier who apparently did not recognize the Kerait leader. Senggum also took flight, but he too was eventually killed in enemy lands.

One group still remained to challenge Temujin's rule: the Naimans. These people had formerly allied with Jamuka against both Temujin and Toghrul, and Temujin launched a campaign against them in approximately the springtime of 1204. Unlike the Keraits, the Naimans were prepared for the conflict. They had a larger force, which included support from the Merkits, Jamuka's Jadirat people, and several other tribes. They were well rested and ready for battle. The Mongol forces, on the other hand, had to travel a long distance to reach their enemy. Temujin's men and horses arrived outside the Naiman camp exhausted.

But one of Temujin's commanders seems to have come up with a clever plan. Setting up camp to recover before attacking, he told the Mongol soldiers to light several fires each. This scheme would give the appearance that the Mongol forces were far more numerous than they actually were.

The plan worked—to a point. A messenger brought word to Tayang, the Naiman army's commander, that the Mongols "have more fires than the stars in the sky." At this news, Tayang wanted to draw back, luring the Mongol army forward to tire them once more. But his son, Kuchlug, thought the move cowardly and berated his father for such weakness. So the battle began, somewhere on the plains and foothills west of modern Ulaanbaatar.

As the fighting got under way, Jamuka withdrew with his men at the last minute. The retreat left Tayang with reduced troops and facing a Mongol force that was better organized than his own. The resulting battle was bloody and devastated the Naiman ranks. Fleeing the scene were the Merkits, whom Temujin's men pursued, battled, and ultimately defeated.

This thirteenth-century Persian manuscript illustration shows two Mongol tribes fighting with lances.

Jamuka, too, soon met his end. Sometime in about 1205 or 1206, Temujin's men caught up to Jamuka. According to *The Secret History*, Temujin confronted the captive and gave his old anda brother a chance to redeem himself and to reforge the bonds between them. He pled with Jamuka,

> Once we moved together like the two shafts of a cart,
> but you thought about separating from me and you left.
> Now that we're together again in one place
> let's each . . . remind the other of what he forgot.

In this version of events, Jamuka declines the offer, claiming that he does not deserve mercy and should be put to an honorable death. Whether this passage in *The Secret History* is based on fact or merely invented by the author as a dramatic story is not known. But two things are certain. As a man who valued loyalty over all, Temujin was probably hurt and angered by what he saw as Jamuka's treachery. And as that traitor, Jamuka was indeed executed. The blood brotherhood was broken once and for all.

ELEVATION

It had been a difficult five or six years. In that time, Temujin had faced down a host of challenges and plots—including from some of the people he had once trusted most. But he had once again gained mastery over the Mongol tribes and more. In the wake of these events, he convened another kurultai. Held on the banks of the Onon River in 1206, this conference reaffirmed his position as khan. But it went a step further. Temujin now took the title of Genghis Khan.

This new name's meaning has never been determined for certain. A common interpretation, however, is that the word *Genghis*—sometimes spelled Chinggis or Chingis—was related to a word meaning "ocean" or "oceanic." Perhaps it implied that Genghis would rule an area as vast as an ocean or that his empire would stretch between oceans. Other historians have translated the title as "strong" or "universal lord." And the exact origin of the title is equally mysterious. It was not in traditional use, as Gurkhan was. Perhaps it had some personal importance, now forgotten, to Temujin. Or maybe it was chosen by a shaman and had a connection to the Mongols' animist faith.

Mongol leaders bring tribute to Genghis Khan, who sits on an ornate throne. This fourteenth-century illustration appears in Rashid al-Din's Collected Chronicles.

FINDING FAITHS

Temujin's conquest of the Keraits, Merkits, and Naimans brought a different religion into his nation. These groups followed Nestorianism. This sect of Christianity is named for its founder, Nestorius. In the A.D. 300s and 400s, Nestorius lived in a region that eventually became Turkey. He believed and taught that Christ was both human and holy but that these two qualities were separate. Not all Christians accepted this idea, but the religion did gain many followers. As it spread, its missionaries (religious teachers) began traveling through Asia. They brought the faith to Mongolia (as well as China) in the seventh and eighth centuries and claimed a large number of followers by the time of Temujin's conquests.

In any case, the title clearly marked the elevation of Temujin to a still higher position. With this elevation came rewards for Genghis's trusted friends and companions. Men such as Borchu, Jelme, and Jebe became commanders and leaders within the Mongol ranks.

The Mongol people now had a single leader. They had found in Genghis Khan a ruler who could restore their former influence and importance on the great Mongolian steppes. And the tribes under his rule included not only a wealth of Mongol clans but also Merkits, Naimans, Keraits, and Tatars. Together, these peoples represented a new Mongol confederation, with Genghis Khan as its head.

CHAPTER FOUR

THE FOUNDATIONS OF AN EMPIRE

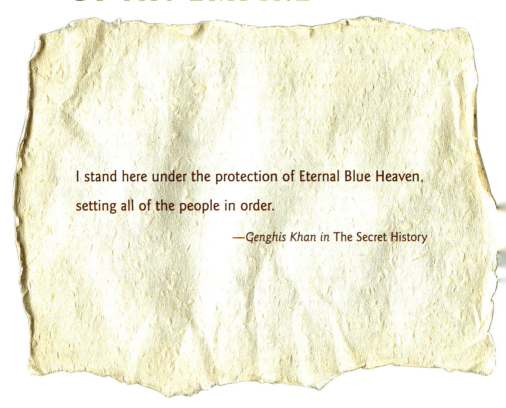

> I stand here under the protection of Eternal Blue Heaven, setting all of the people in order.
>
> —*Genghis Khan in* The Secret History

As khan—both before and after taking the title of Genghis—the Mongol nation's supreme ruler displayed a unique style of leadership. He introduced a number of new measures that were different—and sometimes contradictory—to those of his predecessors. These changes did not always sit well with all of his subjects. But they represented several important shifts.

A NEW ORDER

The Secret History describes in detail how, when Genghis took his new title in the 1206 kurultai, he enumerated dozens of his closest friends and allies and singled out each one for thanks and rewards. According to the *History*, he reminisced with each about their past together and the triumphs and trials that they had shared. Along with these thanks came assignments—specific positions and roles that each man would have in Genghis's new Mongol Empire. For example, Genghis said to his old friend Borchu, "When I was young and thieves stole my eight horses . . . you became my companion for no other reason than the courage in your heart." He went on, "Let [Borchu] rule over the ten thousand people to the south of the Altai, all those people who sleep with the Altai mountains as their pillow."

While these gifts and assignments showed his gratitude to those who had fought, suffered, and succeeded alongside him, they were also extremely practical. By placing his most trusted friends and allies in command, Genghis hoped to ensure great dependability among his top-ranking officers.

In addition, Genghis Khan made a conscious decision not to assign top roles to the former leaders of conquered tribes. By doing so, he demonstrated once again that devotion was more important to him than bloodlines or traditional nobility. But also—and perhaps even more important—he reduced the power held by those groups and their former chiefs and lessened their chances of staging an overthrow or a rebellion against his own authority.

This division of people and duties extended well beyond Genghis's inner circle. His newly assigned commanders took

charge of not only the army but the entire population of the
Mongol realm. Genghis set about dividing all the people of
his nation in a system designed along military lines. All men
of fighting age (probably starting at between fifteen and
twenty years old) were required to serve as warriors. In addition, all were placed in military-style units. The family of a
married man was connected to the same division he was.
Members of the various tribes and clans were generally dis-
persed through different units, unless the tribe in question
was so faithful as to not seem a threat. Like the removal of
tribal chiefs from power, this practice weakened tribal affilia-
tions, aiming to replace these ties with loyalty to Genghis
and the new Mongol nation. Leaving one's assigned unit was
a crime punishable by death.

As part of this reorganization, Genghis Khan introduced
a strict and detailed management of his subjects' roles. This
organization was much more fine-tuned than the systems
used by earlier Mongol leaders. Genghis set about creating
specific jobs and assigning tasks and duties to individuals
and groups among his followers. A large number of these
men were assigned to protect Genghis himself. His body-
guard became an elite and highly trusted unit.

Genghis also went on to create subgroups—both in the
wider Mongol units and in his own guard—in charge of specific tasks such as slaughtering livestock for food. He ordered
that greater attention be given to training horses, with some
tribe members assigned specifically to this task. And he
assigned a group of archers to protect the herds of livestock,
as well as guards to watch over the tribe's precious horses.
Some men were in charge of raising the "Palace Tent," the

khan's large personal ger. He placed others in charge of distributing weapons and other gear to the army.

ARMY ASSETS

By the time Temujin became Genghis Khan, he had spent more than fifteen years of his life as part of an army. Genghis had emerged as a talented military commander. He had begun honing his force's organization and strategy, while also continuing to use many traditional weapons and tactics that had long served Mongol fighters well.

Life on the Mongolian plateau had long been one of frequent raids and battles. Over time the Mongols had developed an array of powerful and effective weapons. For instance, many fighters carried lariats, or lassos, which they swung from horseback to capture or injure enemies. Most warriors also carried a lance—a long wooden pole with a sharp metal point. A Mongol lance also had a curved hook for pulling an

BY THE NUMBERS

Genghis Khan seems to have used an old Asian model to organize his army numerically. This structure was based on multiples of 10, in a decimal system. The largest unit was called a *tumen* and was made up of 10,000 men. Each tumen contained 10 smaller divisions, called *mingghan*, each of which held 1,000 men. Each mingghan was comprised of 10 *jaghun*, which were made up of 100 men each. And each jaghun was made up of 10 *arban*, with 10 men each.

enemy off his horse. Some soldiers also carried heavier weapons such as axes and sabers (curved-blade swords).

The most valuable weapon of all, however, remained the bow and arrow. The Mongols used composite bows, so named because they were made from a combination of materials. Mongol bow makers carefully constructed these weapons from wood, horn (from animals such as deer or water buffalo), sinew (tendons and other tissue from game animals including deer), and glue made from animal products such as the boiled skin and bones of fish. The finished product was both extremely strong and flexible. Mongols also used two different styles of arrows—light, slender ones that were ideal for shooting great distances and heavier, iron-tipped ones better suited to close-range fighting.

Historians believe that a good Mongol bow may have launched light wooden arrows as far as 2,600 feet (800 m) or even farther. In the hands of a talented archer, they could be accurate at distances of about 1,640 feet (500 m). In general, archers on horseback could strike an enemy between 600 and 900 feet (183 and 274 m) away.

A thirteenth-century Chinese artist created this woodcut of a Mongol warrior with saber, lance, and bow.

To protect themselves against the arrows and other weapons of their enemies, Mongol warriors often wore armor made of thick leather strips. This protective gear covered a soldier's chest, back, shoulders, legs, and arms. Soldiers also wore helmets made of metal and leather.

Mongol warriors' horses gave them another advantage over their foes. While Mongols were certainly not the only group to fight from horseback, they were among the best and most skilled. Almost the entire Mongol force was made up of cavalry (soldiers on horseback). They equipped their steeds with high-quality gear, as well. Leather saddles provided comfort, allowing Mongol soldiers to ride further, while stirrups gave Mongol archers much greater control while shooting. And like their riders, horses wore leather armor.

In addition, Mongol forces heading for conflict usually traveled with a large number of remounts. These extra horses were ready to ride when warriors' original steeds grew weary. This practice ensured that a Mongol warrior usually rode a fresh and energetic horse, giving him greater speed and agility. It also allowed the Mongol army to cover large distances very quickly. At times they traveled as far as 200 miles (322 km) in three days.

PLANNING AHEAD

Strategy was just as important as weapons when it came to winning wars on the steppes. The Mongol army used a variety of methods, tricks, and ruses in battle. Genghis Khan was a shrewd military commander, and one of his particular talents proved to be instilling fear and lowering confidence in the enemy long before the fighting even began.

One of Genghis Khan's tactics was to send spies and messengers riding ahead of the army to spread rumors that greatly exaggerated the number of Mongol soldiers on the way. Once Mongol forces actually neared an enemy's camp or city, they sometimes advanced with their men arranged in a wide front, to make numbers look even larger than they were.

Some sources also say that the Mongols constructed life-sized dummies and placed them on the army's extra horses. From even a relatively short distance, these stuffed soldiers looked real enough to fool many foes into thinking the Mongols had far more men than they actually did.

Shamans also played a role in this dance of intimidation. When two Mongol groups faced off, they often sent their shamans to high points near the site of battle. Each side's shamans then beat drums, lit fires, and prayed. If a storm or some other natural event chanced to happen during the lead-up to battle, each side generally tried to claim the happening as a sign of their favor in heaven's eyes.

These ruses were important because, once the Mongol army ventured beyond the familiar Mongolian steppes, it was very often the smaller force in most of its battles. Only superior tactics and strategy could guarantee them the win.

Genghis also placed a high value on gathering very good advance intelligence. His scouts and spies rode out ahead of the army to determine the lay of the land, the number of the enemy, the types of weapons they had, and so forth. With this information, Genghis could decide how best to attack.

Once the battle began, two primary divisions comprised

the Mongol army—both cavalry. A light cavalry was made up of horse-mounted archers who also sometimes carried javelins. Each of these archers could release several arrows in a row, very quickly. These men wore little or no armor, making them light and fast on their mounts. The heavy cavalry, by contrast, usually did wear armor. They carried swords, lances, and sometimes heavier weapons such as axes.

The armored heavy cavalry usually marched into battle first, protecting the light cavalry behind them. As the fighting opened, the light cavalry usually moved up quickly through the ranks to unleash a barrage of arrows at the enemy. They could inflict a great deal of damage on their foes while remaining at some distance from them. In one effective formation, a long line of archers moved to the front of the ranks, launched their arrows, and retreated to be replaced by another long line ready to fire, and so forth. Once the foe had been weakened by the archers' attack, the light cavalry could pull back and let the heavy cavalry take over the battle's closer combat. To guide the soldiers and issue orders during battle, officers sent signals through waving flags or sounding trumpets.

Another typical Mongol strategy was to approach the enemy, wait for them to engage, and then pull back in an apparent—but false—retreat. When the foe pressed forward in pursuit of the Mongols, they were often drawn into an area where they were vulnerable or at a tactical disadvantage. Genghis's troops were also skilled at using the element of surprise. For example, they were sometimes able to attack an unsuspecting enemy by reaching them through a difficult, secret, or otherwise unpredictable route.

Along with adjustments to the army's organization,

Genghis Khan introduced several new policies related to war's aftermath. One regarded the treatment of the tribes he defeated. In the past, when nomadic groups went to war against one another, the victor kept the loot, took a few captives, and in many cases also executed some of the enemy. But the bulk of the defeated people were left among their ruined camp or fled into the wilderness. This practice left the losers plenty of opportunity to regroup, rebuild their strength, and repay their enemies for beating them in the first place. The same two rivals might fight each other over and over again—and so they did, for many decades.

But for Genghis Khan to succeed at uniting the tribes under his rule, this cycle had to stop. So instead of dispersing the groups he conquered, he usually worked to integrate them into his own larger group. While he often executed some of the defeated group's leaders, he generally worked to incorporate most of the defeated people into his growing confederation. Some sources suggest that he took pains not to give the impression that these people were being taken as slaves. Instead, they were to be regarded as new and welcome members of the larger "family" of the Mongol nation.

Genghis also introduced a new system of seizing and distributing loot. Gathering a defeated clan's spoils had always been a major part of steppe conflict. It was one of the main ways in which groups increased their wealth and status. In the past, however, fighters frequently interrupted their attack to begin scooping up their prizes. The result could be an incomplete victory and the escape of enemy leaders. In addition, the loot was far from evenly divided. Every man took what he could carry. Some ended up with nothing.

Genghis Khan apparently realized that his forces would win their battles more decisively if they focused first on the battle and then on the booty. Additionally, he decided to distribute the spoils more fairly among all his men.

RULES AND REGULATIONS

With so many changes, so many subjects, and such a large realm, Genghis needed a system of rules. Otherwise, the typical strife of the steppes might tear his new empire apart.

Mongol society had not been entirely lawless in the past. But it had often been chaotic. In addition, the rules of steppe life were unwritten, and they varied somewhat from group to group. Having absorbed a large number of different clans and tribes into his nation, Genghis needed to standardize these rules. In addition, in order to ensure that they were obeyed throughout his realm, they needed to be set down in writing.

FAMILY MAN

As Genghis Khan's empire expanded and he prepared for future conquests, his family also grew. He and his first wife, Borte, had three more sons after Jochi—Chagatai, Ogodei, and Tolui—as well as several daughters. Genghis also went on to marry additional wives—possibly as many as twenty of them. Most of these women came from conquered groups. Genghis also worked to forge bonds through intermarriage between his family and members of conquered, rival, or allied groups.

This ninth-century book, from Xinjiang in modern China, uses Uighur script to record sermons in the Old Turkic language.

Genghis Khan himself did not read or write, however. Nor did most of his closest associates. But Genghis had chosen a man to help him with the job. In battle against the Naimans, Mongol forces had captured a man named Tatatunga. Of Uighur background, Tatatunga had served as a record keeper for Naiman leaders. His Uighur language was similar enough to the Mongol tongue that Uighur script could be adapted and used to record Mongolian.

Genghis also decreed that his sons and some of his high-ranking officers would learn to read and write Mongolian using this script. Tatatunga himself was likely their tutor.

Overseeing the legal system's creation and enforcement was one of Genghis's adopted brothers, the Tatar Shigi Khutukhu. Genghis decreed, "Shigi Khutukhu will be my eyes for seeing and my ears for hearing. . . . Let no man violate his word." *The Secret History* goes on:

[Genghis Khan] made Shigi Khutukhu the judge of all the people,

commanding him to strike fear in the hearts of thieves,
bring remorse to the tongues of liars,
execute those whom custom has condemned to death,
and punish all those whom custom insists should be
punished.
Genghis Khan made him the judge of all the people,
saying:
"Let him write everything in a blue book,
recording how he's divided the people,
recording how he's judged the people,
and for all generations
let no one change anything Shigi Khutukhu,
after taking counsel with me,
has written on the white paper of his blue book.
Let no man who comes after us alter it."

This set of laws came to be known as the "Great Yasa" or "Book of the Yasa." The book itself—which was actually a number of scrolls—has been lost to the ages, but later sources give us clues about what it contained. It seems to have documented formerly unwritten rules of the steppes, as well as recording Genghis Khan's decrees and laws for his new state. Over time, it seems to have expanded to include the khan's new orders or statements. It may also have contained records of legal events, such as the trials of criminals.

Many of the laws in the Yasa were very strict. Crimes such as robbery and adultery, for example, carried a death penalty. When a person was found guilty of such a crime, his or her entire family was sometimes executed along with the guilty party. But while the Yasa's laws could be harsh, the result does seem to have been a decrease in crime and a general increase in safety among the Mongols during Genghis's reign.

TO EACH HIS OWN

Genghis Khan proved to have a real talent for seeing the individual strengths of his followers and putting them to the best use. For instance, he placed his brother Kassar—always so skilled with a bow and arrow—in charge of a group of archers. By taking into account each commander's individual abilities, he strengthened the potential of his entire people as a nation and a force.

The khan also showed innovation in the way that he assigned status and rank to his followers. He went against traditional practices by elevating people based on their merits and their proven loyalty to him, rather than on their hereditary nobility or familial relationship to him. He gave his faithful friends Borchu and Jelme high positions, for example—higher than the spots he granted to some of his elders and people of more aristocratic birth.

This nontraditional tactic and some of Genghis's other new rules ruffled feathers among those who were used to the old way of doing things. In particular, it irked those who had benefited from those older practices. But the practice was true to the young khan's trait of valuing loyalty above all else—even above family.

And the changes pleased others—especially people of humble birth and traditionally low status. Under the new system, they found that through hard work and, most of all, through unwavering faithfulness to their khan, they could achieve rank and respect. Allegiances often shifted and broke in steppe politics. But Genghis Khan's nontraditional policies seem to have won him unusually faithful followers. Historians believe that, of the khan's trusted inner circle of commanders and companions, none ever betrayed him.

MONGOLIAN PONY EXPRESS

With such a large area to govern and with intelligence such an important part of warfare, Genghis Khan needed quick and efficient communication throughout his empire. With this goal in mind, he created a courier system called the *yam*.

Possibly inspired by similar systems in China, the yam was a group of messengers on horseback who carried news, intelligence, and other messages from one corner of the realm to the other. These riders raced across the steppes, traveling along routes dotted by small stations. These posts were spaced at distances of about a day's ride apart. They provided riders with stops where they could eat and sleep if necessary, as well as mount fresh and well-rested horses. Using this sophisticated network, some riders reportedly covered as many as 200 miles (322 km) a day. Eventually the yam also became useful to traders and other travelers, in part because security along these routes was tight, guarding against raids or other dangers.

CHAPTER FIVE
STORMING THE GATES OF CATHAY

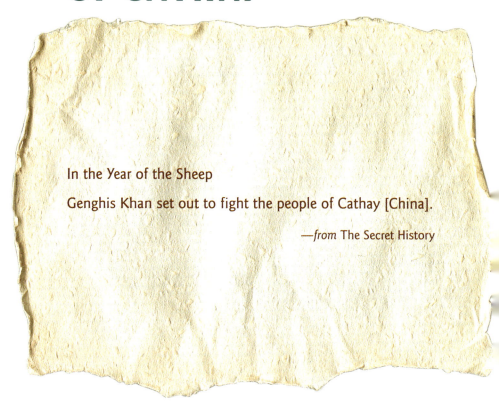

In the Year of the Sheep

Genghis Khan set out to fight the people of Cathay [China].

—*from* The Secret History

At approximately forty years old, Genghis Khan ruled over thousands of families and a vast swath of the Mongolian steppes. In addition, he was the commander of a huge and effective fighting force. He had laid a sturdy foundation for an empire the likes of which the Mongols had never seen before. What next?

Many historians believe that Genghis Khan was shrewd enough to realize that his newly unified Mongols would not remain at peace with one another forever. Without some driving goal to give them a common purpose, the old ways of infighting and rivalry would probably reemerge before long.

Of course, the khan was also probably eager to expand his power and territory even further. Having risen from his early, bleak prospects to the role of Khan of the Mongols must have been exhilarating. Perhaps he was hungry for more. And the riches of other realms offered still another tempting reason to fight. Kingdoms such as those lying southward possessed vast amounts of wealth. Genghis likely thought—probably correctly—that his subjects would be happier and less likely to rebel if they had plenty of spoils to enrich their camps. Whatever his precise motives, Genghis clearly had a variety of reasons to choose his next target: China.

DRAGONS TO THE SOUTH

In the early thirteenth century, China was not a unified nation or empire. Several different ethnic groups, leaders, and dynasties held different parts of this vast area.

One realm within this territory was Xi Xia, which lay across the Gobi from Genghis's lands and north of Tibet. Xi Xia's founders and rulers were not ethnically Chinese. They were Tanguts, a Tibetan-speaking people of the Qiang ethnic group. Most Tanguts were Buddhists. The monk Siddhartha Gautama (Buddha) had founded Buddhism in India in the 500s B.C. The religion had gained widespread influence in China between about the fourth and sixth centuries A.D. Some of Buddhism's central ideas are the search for enlightenment, the renouncement of worldly things, and a life of virtue and wisdom.

East of Xi Xia, the Jin dynasty, ruled by the Jurchen people, controlled a large realm in northeastern China. Like the Tanguts, most Jin subjects were Buddhists. Beginning in the early 1100s, the Jin had become China's most powerful group. As they subdued groups both in China and to the north, they gained in wealth by charging their subjects tribute. This taxlike fee could be paid in various goods or valuables, depending on the particular group's assets.

The Jurchens also dominated the Song dynasty. The Song had once ruled most of eastern China. But their strong suits were cultural and economic advancement, not military prowess, and the Jin overpowered them. By the early 1200s, the Song held only southern China.

Mongol and Jin forces had clashed with each other many times over the previous century or so. In fact, Genghis Khan's ancestor Kabul Khan had fought the Jin in his day. Mongol groups also had a long history of launching raids against settlements in Jin territory.

And the Jin themselves had certainly played a role in steppe politics over the years through their defensive tactic of playing the nomadic tribes against one another. But this practice had not won them many friends among their neighbors. And Jin rulers also struggled with internal tensions and divides.

CRUCIAL CAPITALS

Beijing, China's present-day capital, is located just east of the site of the old Jin capital of Zhongdu.

COMMERCIAL HIGHWAY

One prize of note within the Xi Xia and Jin territories was the Silk Road, a major corridor of trade between Asia and Europe. Many other trade routes passed through the region, as well. Along these courses traveled caravans of merchants carrying a wealth of valuable goods. In addition to the rich silks that gave the Silk Road its name, traders carried spices, furs, porcelain, and jade westward. In exchange for these goods, merchants brought gold, silver, glass, amber, ivory, and other materials from Europe, Persia, and Africa. If Genghis controlled China and thus these routes, he would control not only an invaluable commercial highway but also an important link between eastern and western lands.

Genghis also had supporters among the traders who carried their goods along these routes. Most of them were happy with his rule, because it brought stability to the region through which they had to travel. They also found many new customers among the Mongols, especially those enriched by the spoils of recent conquests.

Marco Polo's caravan on the Silk Road, shown on a map from the Catalan Atlas, a thirteenth-century Majorcan work.

Further complicating life under Jin rule were environ-
mental and weather issues, which had led to problems such
as food shortages. Meanwhile, many of the non-Jurchen
people whom the Jin had conquered chafed under their rule
and saw them as outsiders. The mighty Jin Empire, while
still powerful, was clearly under great strain from within. At
the same time, Xi Xia, the Jin, and all the realms within
China continued to struggle with one another for power,
territory, and influence.

TAKING ON THE TANGUTS

Genghis chose Xi Xia as his first target. While the kingdom
had flourished in the tenth and eleventh centuries, by the
1200s, it was relatively vulnerable compared to the more
powerful Jin. Its armies were smaller, and most of its cities
were less heavily fortified than those of the Jin.
Furthermore, if Genghis were able to conquer this western
area, he could go on to attack the Jin without worrying
about Tangut attacks from behind.

The Xi Xia realm was also quite rich—offering Genghis a
potentially quick and fairly easy source of loot. In addition to
coveting Tangut products such as woven cloth and other
items, the Mongols may have sought more practical prizes.
The Mongols' herds had likely shrunk dramatically during the
years upon years of conflict. Tangut farms and fields could
prove a valuable source of animals to replenish these herds.

The first major attack on Xi Xia—beyond those aiming
only for plunder—seems to have been in 1209. Genghis led
his troops on a march southward, covering more than 600

miles (966 km) and trekking through the Gobi Desert. As they entered Xi Xia territory, they clashed with Tangut troops several times. While each side enjoyed some success, the Tanguts' victories were not enough to stop the Mongols' advance. And that advance was often costly for the Tanguts, as the Mongols plundered the realm's country-side and villages. Having no use nor particular respect for farmland and settlements, the nomadic soldiers often laid waste to the land.

But to reach the heart of Xi Xia and its capital city, Yinchuan, they first had to travel through a narrow mountain pass. Probably in the spring of 1209, the Mongol army reached this pass. Unsurprisingly, they found the important gateway well guarded by thousands of Tangut forces. When a battle ensued, neither side was able to get the upper hand. It seemed as though the fighting might continue for a long time without gaining either side much ground.

Assessing the situation, Genghis commanded his army to use one of their tried-and-true strategies. The Mongol soldiers pretended to retreat, disappearing into the hillsides. They left only a small group of soldiers visible to the Tangut commanders, thus drawing the Tangut soldiers out of their protected position. The ruse worked as well as ever. Lured into the open, the Tanguts suffered a sound defeat as Mongol forces poured out of their hiding places. The Mongol army took the pass and charged onward to Yinchuan.

They ran into serious new challenges when they reached the capital, however. Genghis's army had no real experience taking cities. And as powerful as they were in the combat of the steppes and at hit-and-run raids, those tactics were far less effective when it came to seizing a city. They were even less useful when facing a walled city.

Few details remain about how the Mongols first attempted to breach Yinchuan's walls. But the Tangut commander defending the capital appears to have done a good job of keeping them out, for Genghis's army tried without success for at least two months.

Xi Xia's ruler likely realized that his forces could not keep out the Mongols forever. Looking for help, he reached out to the Jin dynasty. But the Jurchen emperor refused his neighbor's request for aid. The thirteenth-century Chinese historian Yuwen Mozhao reported that the Jin ruler saw no reason to abandon his realm's usual stance toward conflicts beyond the Jin borders. According to Yuwen, the emperor responded, "It is advantageous to my state if its enemies attack each other. What grounds do we have for concern?"

The Tanguts had a stroke of luck in approximately early 1210, when the frustrated Mongols tried a new strategy—an attempt to flood Yinchuan. Sources disagree on how they went about it. Some say that Genghis directed his men to build a dam for this purpose, while others suggest that the Mongols simply broke the walls of the canals already used by the Tanguts to irrigate their fields. However they went about it, the plan backfired. While floodwaters did spread across the plain to Yinchuan, they did not seriously threaten the city's buildings. Floodwaters also streamed into Genghis's own camp, however, where they did cause problems. His troops were forced to seek higher ground, along with their tents, horses, and carts.

Despite this setback for the Mongols, the Tanguts faced

a dilemma. Even if the Mongols were now a bit soggy, they were still at Yinchuan's gates, and the Jin were unwilling to help drive them away. And with his own camp partially underwater, Genghis was willing to negotiate. The two discussed a treaty, of sorts. Genghis agreed to withdraw if the Tanguts gave him troops to add to his army. But Xi Xia's leader declined, claiming that his men were not well suited to nomadic styles of warfare and travel. He offered other riches instead, promising to give Genghis "the great herds of camels who flourish beneath our sheltering trees. We'll give him the woolen clothing and satins we weave. We'll give him the best of the birds we've trained for the hunt." He also presented his own daughter as a wife for Genghis Khan.

Genghis was dissatisfied with the offer—seeking, as usual, new soldiers above all else. However, with his own position weakened, he had little choice but to accept.

PAVING THE WAY TO CATHAY

The Xi Xia were subdued and at least tentatively allied with Genghis through marriage. So he turned his attention to the Jin dynasty.

Genghis had already attracted the Jurchens' attention himself. In about 1208, a new Jin emperor had come to power. Previously, the Mongols had not been among the nations paying tribute to the Jin emperor. But the situation had been muddied by Genghis's defeat of Toghrul and the Keraits, who *had* sent tribute. When the new emperor took the throne, he sent a messenger to Genghis Khan, asking for assurances of the khan's respect. According to legend,

Genghis refused to pay either tribute or respect to the ruler. In fact, he went so far as to spit on the ground while declaring the new emperor to be a weakling—and a stupid one, at that. With this gesture, he essentially declared his intent to challenge the Jin emperor's power.

TOOLS OF THE TRADE

Even after the Xi Xia campaign, the entire idea of seizing permanent settlements was still quite new to nomadic Mongol troops. They still lacked the tools and the know-how to do it effectively.

They did have one method available that required neither new equipment nor special training. The Mongols found that they could simply block routes to and from the city, eventually starving out its inhabitants. But this method could take weeks or even longer—especially against the Jin, whose cities were well stocked with food and other provisions.

Needing new and better tactics, the Mongol army eventually adopted several siege weapons to use in such attacks. Most of these tools were designed by the Chinese themselves, whose war engineers created many sophisticated weapons. They included battering rams for breaking down gates and damaging fortress walls and ladders for scaling those walls. Mongol armies also began using catapults for launching heavy stones over or against city walls. Chinese defectors and captives were often responsible for operating and maintaining these new weapons.

But despite his victories in Xi Xia, Genghis knew better than to rush into an attack on the Jin. Their armies were huge compared to the Mongols' forces—historians estimate that the Jin emperor commanded about 600,000 troops, while Genghis probably had between 75,000 and 100,000, or possibly as few as 50,000. And many Jin cities were heavily fortified with thick walls. But the Jin forces were also spread too thin at the time, due to internal struggles and troubles with Xi Xia and the Song dynasty. The time seemed ripe to make a move against the Jin.

In 1211 Genghis held a kurultai on the banks of the Kerulen River. He called together some of his newest allies, such as the leaders of the Uighur people. While confirming their partnership at the kurultai, he also used the conference to discuss the coming attack on the Jin. One good reason for going to war against them—other than the anticipated spoils—was their long-standing hostile relations with the Mongols themselves.

Genghis also appears to have presented the war as partly on behalf of the related Khitan people. This group lived south of the Gobi and practiced Nestorianism, but they had ethnic ties to the Mongols. For about two centuries prior to the rise of the Jin, Khitans had ruled over a region in northern Manchuria as the Liao dynasty. But like so many other groups in the area, they lost their power to the Jurchens in the early 1100s. Genghis had already made some allies among the Khitans during the Baljuna period. He seems to have suspected that the Khitan might revolt against the Jin—especially if they had Mongol forces backing them up.

Genghis gained his commanders' and allies' support for a

campaign against the Jin. But he still had a few more things to take care of before setting out. For one, he made preparations for keeping things quiet at home. He was not about to risk an uprising in his native steppes while he and the bulk of his army were off in China. To prevent any such trouble, he left several thousand troops behind to keep the peace in his absence.

Finally, before launching this momentous new venture, Genghis Khan took time to ask for protection and approval from a higher power. Persian historian Rashid al-Din writes that the khan climbed a mountain to offer the prayer: "O Eternal Heaven. You know and accept that the [Jin emperor] is the wind which has fanned the tumult, that it is he who began this quarrel. He it was who, without cause, executed . . . the elder relatives of my father and grandfather and I seek to avenge their blood."

GETTING A GLIMPSE

As far as historians know, no portraits, in any form, were done of Genghis in his lifetime. But some descriptions were passed down through the years. A thirteenth-century Chinese writer named Zhao Hong described the ruler. He wrote, "[Genghis Khan] is of tall and majestic stature, his brow is broad and his beard is long. His courage and strength are extraordinary."

A DEADLY CYCLE

In spring 1211, the Mongol army began moving southward. When they reached the northern edge of Jin land, they encountered walls marking the Jurchens' first line of defenses. Fortunately for the Mongols, these defenses were guarded primarily by the Ongut people. Of Turkic background, the Onguts had earlier made ties with Genghis Khan and the Mongols—probably around the time of the stay at Baljuna. To seal the bond between them, Genghis helped arrange marriages between prominent Ongut leaders and his own daughter and granddaughter.

Genghis also had friends among traders in the region. They acted as scouts, bringing him information on the state of Jin defenses. And, as Genghis had hoped, Khitan groups also began coming over to the Mongol side. In 1212 a Khitan leader in southern Manchuria began a revolt. Genghis promptly sent Mongol forces to his aid, and together they quickly took a fortified city in the region.

The Chinese campaign soon settled into a fairly consistent cycle of attacks, counterattacks, retreats, and advances. The Mongol army was still best suited to battle on the steppes. Taking a walled city remained nearly impossible. But as they moved southward, the Mongol forces took a number of towns and cities in northern Jin lands. Many were not well defended. The most heavily fortified cities still stood relatively untouched, as the Mongol army simply passed them by.

Nevertheless, the Mongol advance was enough to make the Jin emperor uneasy. In approximately the summer of 1212, he offered to discuss a treaty, but Genghis refused. Soon afterward, the Mongols gained another critical ally—a diplomat sent by the Jin emperor to negotiate with Genghis. But this officer, Ming Tan, immediately joined the Mongols and offered them insider information on the Jin.

That autumn Genghis and his army launched an attack on Datong, a city in western Jin territory. But when Genghis was wounded in the battle, the Mongols withdrew northward. By the time they regrouped and returned to China in 1213, Jin forces had strengthened their defenses. And so the cycle continued.

Several patterns emerged as the China campaign went on. One was that, when cities surrendered right away—thereby not costing the Mongols any of their soldiers—their inhabitants were generally spared from attack or capture. Those populations who resisted the Mongol onslaught, by contrast, usually paid the price—often with their lives. The cities themselves were often destroyed, as well.

Genghis Khan may have believed that, if he could strike enough terror into his enemy in a blistering attack on one city, that city's neighbors might simply hand themselves over to avoid a similar fate. And that belief seemed to hold true. As word spread of this practice of the Mongols, it does indeed appear that many commanders and civilians saw the wisdom of simply surrendering.

At the same time, Genghis continued to encourage people to leave the Jin for the Mongol side. He welcomed such defectors and generally rewarded them for proclaiming their loyalty and assistance to him. This practice eventually began to perpetuate itself, because the more victories the Mongols won in China, the more people wanted to join them. And while the Mongols suffered some setbacks and defeats at the Jins' hands, they won more often than they lost.

One grim but successful tactic in battles against the Jin seems to have been a relatively new one. When storming a settlement—particularly a walled city—the Mongol army began forcing captives from earlier battles to march ahead of the army. Not only did this make the army look larger, but it also placed non-Mongol prisoners on the front lines of a battle. Usually these unfortunate souls were the kin and comrades of the soldiers they marched toward. Before battles, they served as forced labor for the Mongol army, doing jobs such as filling in moats and weakening city walls. In battle, most of them faced a grisly end, doomed either to attack their own people, be attacked by them, or be trampled by the advancing Mongols behind them.

CAPITALS AND CAPTIVES

In early 1214, the Mongols besieged Zhongdu. That spring Genghis set up a camp outside the city. He had the Jin in a tight spot. Most of the surrounding area had already been taken. And a traitorous Jurchen general had assassinated the Jin emperor a few months earlier, replacing him with a different (but still Jurchen) ruler. While the intrigue did not much affect the war with the Mongols, it did dramatically increase internal tensions among the Jin leaders.

A BROTHER LOST

Genghis's brother Kassar is believed to have died during the China campaigns, probably in late 1213 or early 1214.

An Indian artist of the sixteenth century painted Genghis Khan besieging a Tangut fortress.

But Genghis's people were suffering, as well. The extended campaign had depleted his army's food stores, and his own soldiers were going hungry. As summer approached, many were also sick, possibly due to the heat and humidity of the Chinese climate. With these factors weighing on his forces, Genghis entered negotiations with the Jin emperor. But he appears to have implied to the emperor that his troops could still attack if necessary—and that they would, unless given sufficient incentive not to.

Eager for relief from the siege, the emperor agreed to pay handsomely for peace. He handed over a princess of the Jin dynasty as a wife for Genghis, several hundred children as slaves, approximately three thousand horses, and other valuables. *The Secret History* describes the moment when "the gates of [Zhongdu] were opened and they set out great quantities of gold, silver, satins, and other goods."

As the Mongols headed north for a rest, the Jin emperor moved south. He relocated from Zhongdu to a safer position at the southern Jin capital of Kaifeng. But the move incited rebellion and unrest among the emperor's subjects, who took it as a sign of weakness. The Song dynasty, meanwhile, seems to have considered attacking the Jin in its apparent distress. Although Genghis had probably not planned to return so soon, he seized the opportunity he saw in China's chaos. He sent troops back to Zhongdu, and while its people fought bravely, they could not hold out. In spring 1215, the Mongol forces captured the city. After making sure that they found and seized the city's main prize—a store of imperial Jin treasure—Genghis's army unleashed a wave of destruction on the city. They massacred many of

Zhongdu's inhabitants before setting fires throughout the once-beautiful imperial capital.

The seizure of Zhongdu marked a turning point in Genghis Khan's Chinese campaign. Earlier Mongol attacks on Chinese settlements—against both the Jurchen and the Tanguts—had always been carried out primarily for plunder. Mongol groups had not seriously attempted to hold on to territory in China. But in 1215, Genghis Khan began to shift his goals toward conquest. This new direction appears to have been partly spurred by advice from Genghis's new Khitan and Chinese associates.

In this fourteenth-century Persian illustration from the Collected Chronicles, *Genghis's general Samuqa leads a troop of warriors against the Chinese town of Chengdu.*

But the Jin realm proved difficult to break. China had many millions of inhabitants. Not only could the emperor press them into military service, but they also repopulated many cities that had earlier been defeated. As the Mongol cycle continued, they ended up having to retake cities they'd already conquered.

As the war against the Jin dragged on, Genghis began delegating more of the conflict's leadership to other commanders. His general Samuqa conducted a largely successful campaign in about 1216 and 1217. He reached as far south as the Yellow River, although he was driven back at the capital of Kaifeng. Later responsibility for the war in China went mostly to Muqali, one of Genghis Khan's most trusted generals.

Over the following years, Muqali would win many more battles in the north and would press farther and farther southward. Likely aided by Khitans, Tanguts, and other troops, he eventually reached the Shandong region in the east and neared the borders between the Jin and Song empires to the South.

For the time being, Genghis returned to the Mongolian plateau—possibly for the first time in many months. There he began laying plans for conquests still farther away.

CHAPTER SIX
A WAVE CRASHING WESTWARD

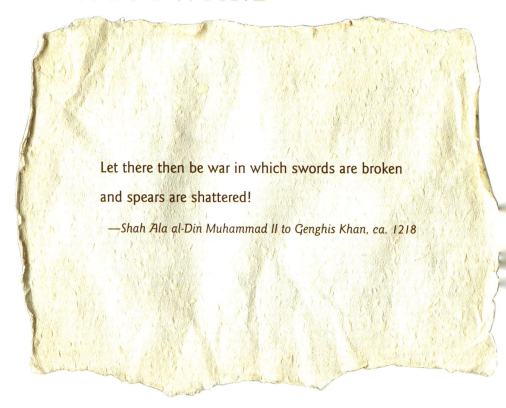

Let there then be war in which swords are broken and spears are shattered!

—*Shah Ala al-Din Muhammad II to Genghis Khan, ca. 1218*

Genghis Khan's focus now turned toward the west. His new target was actually an old enemy—the last major one still remaining.

A YOUNG KINGDOM

The Kara-Khitan realm was located in central Asia, with the heart of its territory comprising an area in modern Kyrgyzstan.

It also included parts of what later became Tajikistan, southern Kazakhstan, and a sliver of western China. A Khitan leader—expelled from his own Manchurian lands by the Jin—had founded the kingdom in the 1100s. He was joined by a population of several tens of thousands of his fellow Khitan people. They gradually created a powerful empire, gaining power over several groups in the area and claiming them as their vassals (subordinate states and peoples). These groups included the Uighurs and Karluks (a nomadic Turkic tribe related to the Uighurs), as well as the Khwarazm kingdom to the west.

Most inhabitants of Kara-Khitan were Muslims, followers of Islam. The prophet Muhammad had founded this religion on the Arabian Peninsula (in modern Saudi Arabia) in the A.D. 600s. Muslims obey the Five Pillars of Islam, which instruct them to declare their faith, to pray, to fast, to give to the poor, and to make a pilgrimage to Mecca (Islam's holy city). The holy text of Islam is the Quran.

By the early 1200s, a Naiman leader named Kuchlug had taken over the rule of Kara-Khitan. Kuchlug had fought the Mongols before, having been driven out of his Naiman lands by Genghis himself about fifteen years earlier. After fleeing westward, he had taken shelter in Kara-Khitan, where he and some of his fellow Naimans became new vassals of the Gurkhan. Kuchlug went on to marry the Gurkhan's daughter and—hungry for power—soon began laying plans to take over the realm himself. He eventually teamed with the leader of the neighboring Khwarazm Empire to defeat the Gurkhan. After a resounding victory over the Kara-Khitan ruler, the Khwarazm ruler and Kuchlug divided the Gurkhan's territory between them.

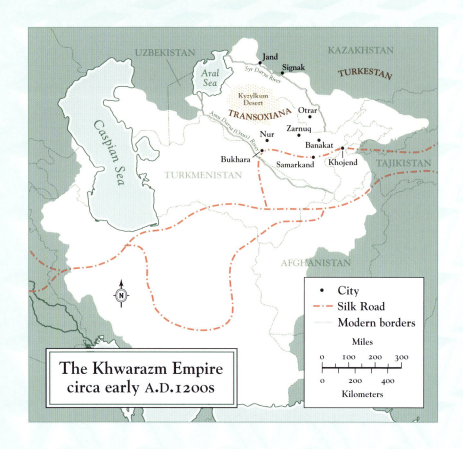

The Khwarazm Empire
circa early A.D. 1200s

A VULNERABLE ENEMY

In about 1217 or 1218, Genghis decided it was time to conquer Kuchlug once and for all. Had Kuchlug simply faded
into the background after the Mongols' earlier defeat of the
Naimans, he might not have become a target of Genghis's
armies. But as the leader of a fairly sizable realm, he posed a
potential threat to the Mongol Empire. Furthermore,
Genghis could not risk the possibility that Kuchlug might
also gather his scattered fellow Naimans together and repay
the Mongols for that prior defeat.

In moving against Kuchlug, Genghis had several important advantages. For one, he already had allies within the Kara-Khitan realm. A group of Uighur, for instance, had pledged loyalty to him in 1209. And Genghis had also learned of a significant internal weakness of Kuchlug's realm. Although most of the native Kara-Khitan people were Muslims, Kuchlug was a Buddhist. He had only recently converted to Buddhism, having been raised (like most Naimans) as a Nestorian Christian. He pursued his new faith with great intensity—so great, in fact, that he decided to thrust it upon his Muslim subjects. He banned public Islamic ceremonies and tortured and executed one Muslim cleric who refused to obey the new rules. Unsurprisingly, Kuchlug's subjects—who already saw him as an outsider—deeply resented this religious persecution.

Given all of these factors, Genghis did not expect too much resistance in the takeover of Kara-Khitan. In fact, he had such confidence that he decided not to take part in the campaign himself. He placed his commander Jebe in charge of the operation and sent him westward with approximately twenty thousand troops.

To reach Kara-Khitan, Jebe and his forces had to cross the Altai Mountains. It was a long and difficult journey, but when they arrived, they found that Genghis's expectations had been correct. As a first move, Jebe apparently announced that Genghis Khan's policy was to respect native religions and allow every person to follow the faith of his or her ancestors. Upon hearing these welcome words, Kara-Khitan residents promptly erupted in a rebellion against Kuchlug and his forces. The Uighurs and Karluks also entered the fray. Kuchlug quickly fled but could count on precious few friends to hide him from the pursuing Mongols. After a chase estimated to cover more than 300 miles (483 km), Jebe's forces caught, killed, and beheaded Kuchlug. They displayed his head to the people of Kara-Khitan, who appear to have viewed the Mongols as liberators from Kuchlug's oppression. This victory essentially ended the Kara-Khitan khanate—and eliminated Genghis's final major foe among the nomadic tribes of the steppes.

NEW NEIGHBORS

The Mongol defeat of Kuchlug brought the borders of Genghis's empire into contact with those of Khwarazm, which lay west of the former Kara-Khitan realm. Khwarazm lay in a region that had been fought over for centuries and had belonged to many different powers during that time. The Khwarazmid Empire itself had emerged in the 1000s. It was one of the most powerful realms in Asia until the mid-1100s, when it fell under the influence of Kara-Khitan. While its boundaries shifted many times over the years, by the 1200s, it stretched from the western edge of modern Tibet, across central Asia to the Caspian Sea. It extended northward to Turkistan, and to the south, it encompassed much of modern Iran and reached to the Arabian Sea. This large realm centered on the Amu Darya River, known as the Oxus in ancient times. This important waterway begins just west of China, flows westward along the modern borders of Tajikistan and Afghanistan, and then turns northward through Turkmenistan and Uzbekistan toward the Aral Sea.

Within this territory lay several important cities and centers of culture and trade, including Bukhara and Samarkand (both in modern Uzbekistan). The Silk Road cut through Khwarazm land, as well.

Many of Khwarazm's inhabitants were ethnically Persian. Like the Kara-Khitan, the realm was primarily Islamic. In fact, the region was roughly part of a mostly Islamic region, which had evolved as Islam spread rapidly outward from the Arabian Peninsula in the 600s. This wide Islamic realm grew very rich, and subgroups fought among themselves for power and territory. But throughout the area, education, culture, and science had flourished.

A GRAVE MISTAKE

In the early 1200s, the Khwarazm Empire's leader was Shah Ala al-Din Muhammad II, often called simply the Khwarazm-shah. (In many Islamic areas, "shah," like the Mongols' "khan," was a title for a ruler.) Historians are unsure whether Genghis initially planned to go to war against the Khwarazm realm. There is little information about his intent, and the few sources available frequently conflict with one another. What does seem clear is that the two rulers sent ambassadors back and forth several times and that they discussed the possibility of a peaceful trade agreement between their realms.

In any case, Muhammad was probably somewhat mistrustful of the khan, who had taken over so much territory in less than three decades and whose successes were by that time well known in the region. In addition, the shah was an unpopular and inept ruler. Sometime between 1217 and 1219, whether due to suspicion, foolishness, or some combination of factors, the Khwarazm-shah had made a fatal move.

In that year, a group of Muslim traders traveled from Genghis's Mongol territories to the city of Otrar, located along Khwarazm's eastern border. When they arrived, the city's governor suspected them of being spies for the Mongol khan—which they may well have been. The governor—perhaps with the shah's knowledge or even at his decree—ordered Khwarazm forces to kill all the merchants and to seize their goods.

When Genghis Khan heard what had taken place, he was furious. But rather than charging directly into battle, it appears that he tried to settle the matter peacefully. Genghis sent three ambassadors to Muhammad to demand he make amends for these deaths. But the shah responded only with further outrages. He put at least one of these envoys to death. The other two may also have been killed or may have had their beards or heads shaved—a terrible insult in Mongol culture.

Rashid al-Din reports that Genghis exploded in fury when he learned of his envoys' fates, saying, "The Khwarazm-shah is no king, he is a bandit!" *The Secret History* quotes Genghis as saying, "How did the [Muslims] break my golden reins? I'll go to war with them to get satisfaction for this crime."

THE QUESTION OF SUCCESSION

Genghis Khan prepared to launch a major offensive against Khwarazm. But one of Genghis's wives urged him to think about his future before setting out for the distant lands. He was, after all, in his fifties—already a fairly advanced age for a Mongol at the time. Life on the steppes was hard—especially on a man who had spent so many years at war. According to *The Secret History*, Yesui, a wife from the Tatar people, said,

> The Khan will cross high mountain passes,
> cross over wide rivers,
> waging a long war far from home.
> Before he leaves has he thought about setting his
> people in order?
> There is no eternity for all things born in this world.
> When your body falls like an old tree
> who will rule your people,
> these fields of tangled grasses?

Genghis agreed, admitting, "I've been sleeping like I won't someday be taken by death." He turned to his four sons to discuss the question of who would follow him as the khan of the Mongols.

At this point, the uncertainty surrounding Jochi's father came back to haunt Jochi. Chagatai supposedly declared that his brother—or perhaps half brother—might actually be the son of a Merkit and therefore should not be Genghis Khan's heir. Genghis angrily defended his eldest son, berating Chagatai for speaking that way about his brother. But—perhaps suspecting that others might raise the same objection to Jochi—Genghis ultimately chose Ogodei to inherit the title of khan. As for the vast empire, all four sons would receive

This sixteenth-century Turkish illustration shows Genghis Khan dividing his empire among his four sons.

territory to oversee. Genghis told them, "Mother Earth is broad and her rivers and waters are numerous. Make up your camps far apart and each of you rule your own kingdom."

AGAINST THE SHAH

With the matter of his heir settled, Genghis prepared to retaliate against Shah Muhammad. Before leaving, he gathered additional soldiers from his Khitan, Chinese, and Uighur allies. He also requested men from Xi Xia, but the Tangut leader refused. *The Secret History* relates that one of the Tangut king's advisers said of Genghis's request, "If he's not strong enough to conquer the [Muslims] alone then why does he call himself khan?" While the response angered Genghis, he did nothing about it for the time being. Settling the score with Shah Muhammad had to come first.

Genghis's combined forces formed one of the largest armies he had yet traveled with. Historians estimate that it comprised between 100,000 and 200,000 men, as well as many thousands of horses. It probably also included some siege weapons, along with engineers who could build other siege weapons as needed. Together they set out toward Khwarazm in 1219. With Genghis Khan were all four of his sons and many of his top generals. The journey covered more than 1,500 miles (2,414 km). Along the way, Genghis's engineers and laborers built roads and bridges to help the army cross mountain ranges, rivers, and other challenging terrain. Steadily they advanced toward the shah and his kingdom.

The Khwarazm-shah must have known that after the murder of the traders and envoy Genghis and his army would be on their way. But he also knew that he was at an extreme disadvantage. Many of his subjects disliked him, and his troops were not absolutely loyal to him. One reason was his ethnicity—unlike most of his subjects, he was Turkish rather than Persian. In addition, he had heavily taxed his population, while he lived in luxury. And the killing of Muslim merchants had not helped his cause, since he and most of his subjects were also Muslims.

Muhammad decided to deploy most of the army among the realm's fortified cities. He knew that the Mongols were still less effective against such settlements than in open areas. He also believed that his troops would find it harder to defect or revolt if they were separated and confined to cities.

As usual, however, Genghis was better informed than his foe, having already gathered a large amount of intelligence through his network of spies, scouts, and allies. He was aware that the shah's army was spread thinly. He also realized that many of the troops were likely to desert Muhammad to save themselves. And he knew the lay of the land in some detail.

Taking all these factors into consideration, Genghis

devised a cunning strategy. He chose to attack the shah's army from multiple directions almost simultaneously, through a three-pronged attack. When Genghis's troops reached Khwarazm's eastern borders in autumn of 1219, Genghis split it into three main groups. An attack on Otrar—the site of the merchants' murders—was one of the first priorities, and Genghis appointed Chagatai and Ogodei the commanders of this mission.

Meanwhile, Genghis sent troops under Jochi to the Syr Darya River. There Jochi's division split in two. One group went northward to Signak and Jand, and the other traveled south along the river toward Banakat and Khojend.

Finally, Genghis himself, along with his son Tolui, set his sights on Bukhara—one of Khwarazm's largest and richest cities. Heading southwest, Genghis's division crossed the Kyzylkum, a wide desert between the Amu Darya and Syr Darya rivers. It was a grueling route and one that few travel-

NOT AGAIN

The Khwarazm kingdom included a region known as Transoxiana. Its name literally meaning "across the Oxus," the area encompassed parts of present-day Uzbekistan, Tajikistan, and Kazakhstan. The arrival of the Mongol armies in Transoxiana did not mark the region's first such invasion. In fact, the area had been taken by one of the world's most famous conquerors before Genghis—Alexander the Great. In the 300s B.C., Alexander's forces had added Transoxiana to their conquests.

Invasion Routes in Khwarazm Empire, A.D. 1219–1220

KAZAKHSTAN

UZBEKISTAN

Jand
Signak
Syr Darya River
TURKESTAN

Aral Sea

Kyzylkum Desert
TRANSOXIANA
Otrar

Amu Darya River

Nur
Zarnuq
Banakat
Bukhara
Khojend
Samarkand
TAJIKISTAN

Caspian Sea

TURKMENISTAN

AFGHANISTAN

Miles
0 100 200 300
0 200 400
Kilometers

— Genghis's route
--- Jochi's route
═ Chagatai's route
• City
--- Modern borders

N

PAKISTAN

ers ever took, which was probably exactly why Genghis chose it. By doing so—and especially while sending Jochi looping around in the opposite direction—he would encircle much of a region in Khwarazm called Transoxiana and would likely surprise the foe.

Genghis's division crossed the frozen Syr Darya in early 1220 and moved through the cities of Zarnuq and Nur. Neither settlement put up much of a fight, and both were taken relatively peacefully. The army pressed on and reached Bukhara in the early spring of 1220.

"PUNISHMENT OF GOD"

Just outside of Bukhara, the Mongols met an initial attack from the city's defensive troops. They defeated the Bukharan force quite quickly, after which the bulk of the city's inhabitants surrendered. There remained, however, a contingent of soldiers who retreated into the city's citadel (fortress) and continued to hold out. They fought bravely, but after several days of siege, Genghis's forces took the citadel.

According to many sources, Genghis went into the defeated Bukhara himself—an unusual event. Until this point, it appears that Genghis rarely entered the cities his army took. His soldiers handled the plundering, captive taking, and execution, while the khan himself stayed in more open areas outside. Genghis—and, in fact, most nomadic Mongols—had a general distaste for city life, seeing the inhabitants of permanent settlements as the inmates of self-made prisons. Why anyone would choose such a life was almost incomprehensible to many nomads.

But perhaps Genghis Khan saw Bukhara as a good place to send a message to the Khwarazm-shah's subjects. A famous story recounts that Genghis gathered the city's richest and most prominent citizens around the central mosque (Islamic place of worship). There, according to Juvaini, he proclaimed: "O people, know that you have committed great sins, and that the great ones among you have committed these sins. If you ask me what proof I have for these words, I say it is because I am the punishment of God. If you had not committed great sins, God would not have sent a punishment like me upon you."

Whether Genghis actually delivered this dramatic speech is unknown. But he certainly did punish the city. His men

In this Persian illustration from 1397, Genghis Khan addresses the people of Bukhara from the steps of the city mosque.

drove out the city's inhabitants and, with plenty of room to move, thoroughly plundered Bukhara's ample stores of wealth. They also killed most of the city's soldiers and some of its other men—after, that is, they'd taken possession of those who could be useful. They carefully identified and separated the skilled artisans who would be sent to Mongolia, the women and children who would be taken as slaves, and those men who would be used by the army as laborers or human shields in the next major battle. Amid the chaos, the city's many wood buildings caught fire, while many of its stone structures had crumbled under the army's assault.

Genghis next advanced on Samarkand, the shah's capital. He and his men met up with Chagatai, Ogodei, and their troops. They had successfully taken Otrar, as well as annihilated the city and captured the governor for eventual execution. Together—and with hundreds of their new captives in the lead—the Mongols surrounded Samarkand and laid siege to it. The heavily defended capital boasted many troops, a moat, thick walls, and a citadel. But when an offensive attack by the city's soldiers failed disastrously, resulting in many casualties, the citizens surrendered. They were then treated similarly as those at Bukhara, while the city's treasuries were looted.

About this time, horrified by the devastation the Mongols were wreaking on his kingdom, Muhammad took flight. He fled westward into a region known as Khorasan and toward the Caspian Sea. Genghis sent a division commanded by Jebe and Subodei (one of the khan's most talented generals) in pursuit of the shah.

Meanwhile, in approximately autumn 1220, Jochi's troops reached the city of Gurganj (known as Urgench, in modern Uzbekistan). This important hub of trade lay near the Amu Darya River delta. Ogodei and Chagatai soon moved to meet Jochi there, and together they laid siege to Gurganj.

This siege would prove one of the longest and hardest the Mongols faced in Khwarazm. The city's position in marshland gave the attackers no stones to launch with their catapults. Arguments between Jochi and his brother Chagatai over how to conduct the mission may have slowed down the operation further. And the city's inhabitants fought back fiercely.

But the Mongols took their time, putting captives to work filling in the city's moats and attempting to weaken its walls. Fire was the final step, and the siege finally ended in spring 1221. Exhausted and frustrated, the Mongols laid waste to this city and killed many of its people.

A TIDE OF TERROR

As Genghis's army charged on through Khwarazm, they unleashed a greater level of terror on the land than on any of their earlier conquests. Thousands upon thousands died. Some estimates of the death toll in Khwarazm alone reach the millions. Tens of thousands more became prisoners. Mongol soldiers raped women and tore children away from their parents to make them captives. Once-great cities were left as little more than piles of rubble and charred wood.

What were the reasons for these new and terrifying heights of destruction? Part of the answer may lie in the utter unfamiliarity of these lands to Genghis and his men. As they had shown in China, he and most of his fellow Mongols lacked respect for and understanding of settled city life. And some observers suggest that Genghis originally had no intention of occupying the Khwarazm lands and therefore felt free to leave them in ruins.

But overall, hate and simple bloodthirstiness do not seem to have motivated the Mongols' actions. Instead, most historians and military experts believe that the terror in Khwarazm (and, to a lesser degree, in China) was part of a brutal but effective military strategy. As a relatively small army surrounded by its enemies, inspiring fear was the most efficient way to prevent uprisings, resistance, attacks from the rear, and revolts ahead. This theory is supported by the fact that, following many major attacks, Genghis sent messengers to spread the word of the defeated city's fate through the surrounding country. These morbid bulletins must have served as dire warnings to those who received them.

Whatever drove Genghis's actions and those of his army, it is clear that certain cities received harsher treatment than others. Many of those whose people and troops resisted were virtually destroyed. Even greater punishment was dealt to those in locations where Genghis lost a family member at enemy hands. For example, in March or April of 1221, Mongol forces commanded by Tolui descended on the Persian city of Nishapur. Approximately one year earlier, one of Genghis's sons-in-law had been killed there. Tales of the bloodbath at Nishapur were ghastly. Genghis apparently let his widowed daughter determine the city's fate. The bereaved woman was said to have demanded that every living thing in the city be killed. According to some accounts, the Mongol soldiers even slaughtered the city's cats and dogs. Horror stories told of pyramid-like piles made from the heads of women, children, and men.

A terrible fate also awaited Bamiyan, in Afghanistan. Genghis's grandson Mutugen, a son of Chagatai, was killed in battle at this city. In about 1221, the Mongol army descended on Bamiyan's valley and destroyed the city.

In autumn 1221, the Mongols suffered one of their very few defeats. The loss took place near Kabul (in present-day Afghanistan) at the hands of Shah Muhammad's son Jalal al-Din. Jalal was an apparently talented commander who had succeeded in gathering some troops around him. The uncommon victory gave people in the area some desperately needed hope, and uprisings broke out in several cities. Mongol troops

Only ruins remain of the city of Bamiyan after Genghis Khan's attack in retaliation for the death of his grandson.

put down these revolts and harshly punished the cities and people involved—leveling the city of Heart and killing most of its inhabitants, for example. Meanwhile, Genghis himself rode along in pursuit of Jalal. After chasing him through what later became Pakistan, the Mongols caught up with Jalal in late 1221 by the banks of the Indus River. A brief battle ensued, in which the Mongol forces dominated. When Jalal escaped by crossing the river, Genghis apparently briefly considered following and venturing into India. But the Mongols soon found that the hot climate of the region was devastating not only to their health but also to their weapons and their horses. Genghis turned back.

THE GREAT RAID

While Genghis and most of his army carried on the campaign in central Asia, Subodei and Jebe continued their pursuit of

Muhammad. But around the winter of 1220, Muhammad had reached the Caspian Sea and took shelter on a small island in the sea. Soon afterward, he fell ill and died there, without having been found by Genghis's men. When they heard the news and realized their hunt no longer had any prey, they hesitated to turn back. Having come this far already—and having met relatively little resistance along the way—they wished to press onward into northern lands.

In approximately early 1221, the two generals received permission from Genghis to turn northward. With a force that probably numbered about twenty thousand men, they moved along the western side of the Caspian. They soon entered lands that later became Armenia and Azerbaijan but were then part of Georgia. This kingdom was then at its largest and most powerful, covering much of the southern Caucasus (a region lying between the Caspian and Black seas). Under the skillful reign of Queen Tamar (who ruled from 1184 to 1213), the nation had gained much territory and grown rich from trade. It had also experienced a golden age of progress in culture, arts, and sciences. And Georgia was notable for being one of the oldest Christian states in the world, having adopted the still-young religion in the A.D. 300s.

Subodei and Jebe arrived in Georgian territory looking mainly for loot and for information. But a contingent of the kingdom's army soon confronted them, and a battle between the forces began south of Tbilisi (modern Georgia's capital). Although the Georgian forces were talented and experienced, they were not experienced at fighting the Mongols. In fact, they were not even sure just who the Mongols were. With more knowledge of their enemies and with unexpected tactics, the Mongols took the victory in about February 1221.

Subodei and Jebe continued onward to the north, sending information-gathering scouts, translators, and spies ahead of them. In the plains beyond the Caucasus (in modern-day Russia), the Mongols encountered the Kipchak tribes. These nomadic Turkic peoples (also called the Polovtsy or the Kumans) were a powerful group. And with similar fighting styles and weapons to the Mongols, they were a more formidable foe than the unprepared Georgians.

As the Mongols advanced, probably in autumn 1221, the Kipchaks may also have joined with other tribes in the area to launch attacks on the invaders. In any case, acutely aware of the dangers, Jebe and Subodei reached out to the Kipchaks with a proposal. Apparently through some combination of offering them a share of plunder and noting their similar lifestyles and ethnic ties, they convinced the Kipchaks to keep peace.

But the offer was a ruse. After the Kipchaks had accepted it, the Mongols attacked and the Kipchaks took flight. Mongol troops pursued and killed many of them before moving toward the Dnieper River, which flows north to south and empties into the Black Sea in Ukraine.

At some point around this time, the army—or at least part of it—ventured into the Crimea, a peninsula in the northern Black Sea. The area was a major hub of trade, and the Mongols took the opportunity to loot several rich Crimean port cities.

They had not heard the last of the Kipchaks, however. One of that tribe's leaders called on a Russian prince,

Mstislav Mstislavich of Galich. Russia was not then a united nation but a realm of individual city-states ruled by princes who often battled one another for influence and territory. The Kipchaks were not their allies by any means, either. But in the face of this advancing Mongol threat, all of these parties agreed to join forces temporarily and repel the invaders. Another important member of the coalition was Mstislav Romanovitch of Kiev. He ruled Kievan Rus, a powerful state centered on the Ukrainian city of Kiev. Other princes and troops joined them.

When Jebe and Subodei learned of this partnership, they sent a group of ambassadors to the Russian leaders. Their conflict was with the Kipchaks, not the Russians, they said. If the princes left the coalition, they and their people need not be involved in the clash at all.

The Russians mistrusted the Mongols and their ambassadors, however. Apparently not aware of Shah Muhammad's folly, the Russians executed the ambassadors.

This action, of course, guaranteed war. The conflict began at the Dnieper in approximately spring 1222. With a much larger number of men, the Mongols' foes enjoyed some early success. So Jebe and Subodei drew back, moving their men eastward. The Russians and Kipchaks gave chase, and as the pursuit dragged on for more than a week—the Mongols staying just out of reach—some of the coalition's divisions fell behind. Jebe and Subodei finally halted at the Kalka River near the Sea of Azov (in Ukraine) and prepared to fight again.

The Battle of the Kalka River began in the spring—probably in May of 1222. While the Mongols were still facing a much larger force, those forces had been spread out by the chase. And the Russians' and Kipchaks' coalition army, however—cobbled together from a group of rivals—lacked communication and organization, not to mention any particular unity. The Mongols saw their opportunity and attacked in full force.

The result was an utter rout, with the Russians and Kipchaks retreating in chaos, running into their own camp and also into the slower troops who were still arriving. The disastrous confusion that resulted was deadly. The few survivors fled, but the Mongols did not let all of them go without a fight. They caught up with Prince Mstislav of Kiev and several other leaders, who then surrendered—expecting to be spared. But the death of the khan's ambassadors was, as ever, a death sentence. The Mongol generals captured Mstislav and his allies and killed them in a way that technically shed no blood. (Bloodless executions, in

Jebe (on white horse) *charges forward at the Battle of the Kalka River in this nineteenth-century painting.*

Mongol culture, were reserved for nobles.) Tying up the Russians and placing them under a ger floor, the Mongols then celebrated their victory with a feast in that very ger— slowly crushing their captives to death.

Jebe and Subodei now began one final march. They moved up the Volga River (in modern-day Russia) into a region known as Volga Bulgaria. This land was home to the Bulgars, a seminomadic people thought to be of Turkic background. But in a resulting clash, the Bulgars showed themselves to be fierce foes. Few details of the conflict remain. Known as the Battle of Samara Bend, it probably took place in late 1222. What is certain is that the Bulgars handed the Mongols another of their few defeats.

Jebe and Subodei didn't stay to suffer another loss. They turned southward again and met up with Genghis and the rest of the army in lands east of the Syr Darya River, in approximately early 1223. Genghis had spent much of late 1222 and early 1223 in the Transoxiana region. Probably in the spring of 1223, he and many of his soldiers took something of a vacation to celebrate their victories. Genghis arranged a massive and months-long battue for tens of thousands of his men.

Jebe and Subodei's arrival completed a raid that is remembered as one of history's boldest and most astonishing. Following a route more than 4,500 miles (7,242 km) long, passing through more than a half dozen countries by modern maps and commanding a relatively small force, Jebe and Subodei had lost only one major battle. The tales of this expedition fueled rumors that Genghis Khan and his armies were invincible.

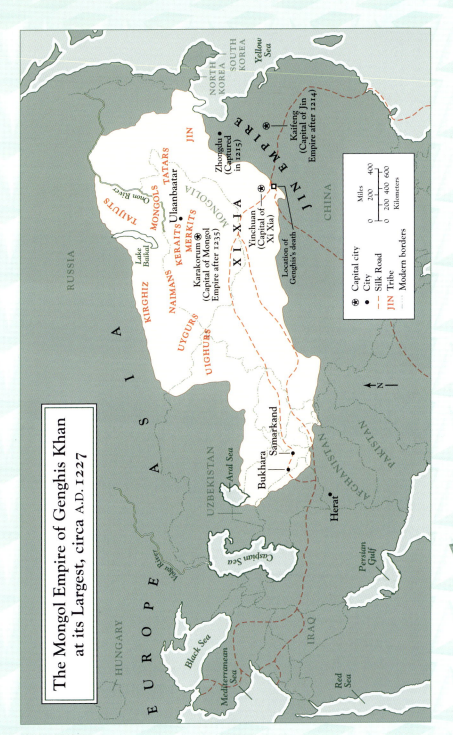

The Mongol Empire of Genghis Khan at its Largest, circa A.D. 1227

RUSSIA

EUROPE

ASIA

HUNGARY

Volga River

Black Sea

Mediterranean Sea

Caspian Sea

Red Sea

IRAQ

Persian Gulf

Aral Sea

UZBEKISTAN

Bukhara

Samarkand

Herat

AFGHANISTAN

PAKISTAN

Lake Baikal

Onon River

KIRGHIZ

NAIMANS

UYGURS

UIGHURS

KERAITS

MERKITS

Karakorum
(Capital of Mongol
Empire after 1235)

MONGOLS

TAIJIUTS

TATARS

Ulaanbaatar

MONGOLIA

JIN

XI XIA

Yinchuan (Capital of
Xi Xia)

Location of
Genghis's death

Zhongdu
(Captured
in 1215)

Kaifeng
(Capital of Jin
Empire after 1214)

JIN EMPIRE

CHINA

NORTH
KOREA

SOUTH
KOREA

Yellow
Sea

Legend	
⊛	Capital city
●	City
– – –	Silk Road
JIN	Tribe
‥‥‥	Modern borders

Miles
0   200   400

Kilometers
0   200   400   600

N

With that remarkable army back together, Genghis Khan made preparations to leave the former lands of the shah. Stationing several divisions to oversee the conquered areas and loading his carts with loot, he headed homeward in about autumn of 1223.

LAST ACT

The journey back to Mongolia was a long one and took many months. After years away, the victorious army finally returned home in about spring 1225. Their arrival was no doubt celebratory, but for Genghis, it was also tinged with sadness. His eldest son, Jochi, did not return with him, having chosen to stay behind in the conquered lands, near the Caspian Sea. Two of Genghis's greatest generals—Jebe and Muqali—had died. And the khan was growing old himself.

Yet Genghis did not stay put for long. He had not forgotten the Tanguts' refusal to send troops for his campaign against the Khwarazm. In addition, Xi Xia was rebuilding its ties with the Jin leaders—still struggling to fight off the Mongols themselves. If the Tanguts regrouped and gained strength, they would pose a grave danger to Genghis's empire. He couldn't take that risk.

Probably in either autumn 1225 or spring of the following year, Genghis returned to Xi Xia with his troops. Once again, they traveled across the Gobi and entered Xi Xia from the west.

As they had so many times before, Genghis's army began laying siege to the kingdom's cities, such as Khara-Khoto and Ganzhou. Some fell quickly, while others required extended assault, but the Mongols' usual tactics were as successful as ever, and the troops advanced steadily. In approximately autumn 1226, they crossed the wide, swift Yellow River. They defeated the city of Lingzhou and finally came to the capital, Yinchuan. As they dug in for what would be a long siege there, some troops—possibly including Genghis himself—moved onward toward Jin territory.

Meanwhile, the old khan's health had begun to fail. At some point in the previous few months, he had fallen from his horse during a hunt. The injuries from this fall had apparently caused a fever, and the unknown illness that gripped Genghis in 1227 may have been related.

MOURNFUL MESSAGE

While at war in Xi Xia, Genghis Khan learned that his son Jochi had died earlier in 1227. Jochi had never returned to Mongolia.

Perhaps sensing that his end was near, Genghis issued some final orders. According to Rashid al-Din, he told his officers, "Do not let my death be known. Do not weep or lament in any way, so that the enemy shall not know anything about it. But when the ruler of the Tanguts and the population leave [Yinchuan] . . . annihilate them all." He also gave his son Tolui and some other commanders advice on how best to defeat the Jin Empire once and for all.

But Genghis himself would not see that campaign. Xi Xia was to be his final battlefield. In the late summer of 1227, Genghis Khan died. He was about sixty-six years old.

Genghis's top officials took his decree of secrecy very seriously. In fact, they were so keen to follow it that, while transporting the khan's body back to Mongolia, they reportedly killed anyone who happened to see the procession as it made its way homeward. Oddly, even *The Secret History* has very little to say. It closes the great conqueror's life with only a simple note: "In the Year of the Pig, Genghis Khan ascended to Heaven."

Mourners carry Genghis Khan's gold and silver coffin as officers kill bystanders who might tell others of his death. An Indian artist created this painting around 1603.

"THE SUNNY SIDE OF THE MOUNTAIN"

Erdeni-yin Tobchi is a long chronicle of Mongol history, written by a Mongolian historian named Sagang Sechen in the 1660s. While not a primary source, it is one of relatively few surviving Mongolian-language works, although it is also a highly creative and sometimes even fantastical work. One chapter of the chronicle focuses on Genghis's death. It describes important officials and family gathering around the bed of the ailing old khan, his death, and finally his burial:

> With his queens and his sons at the head of the procession
> and everyone weeping and wailing from grief,
> they raised his golden body from its place on the cart
> and were unable to carry it any farther.
> They erected an eternal stone marker
> and built around it eight white houses for prayer and
>   offerings.
> Then they buried the Lord's golden body
> on the sunny side of the mountain known as Kentei Khan,
> at the place known as Yeke Oteg.
> Here his eternal name . . .
> lives to the present day.

EPILOGUE
In the great khan's wake

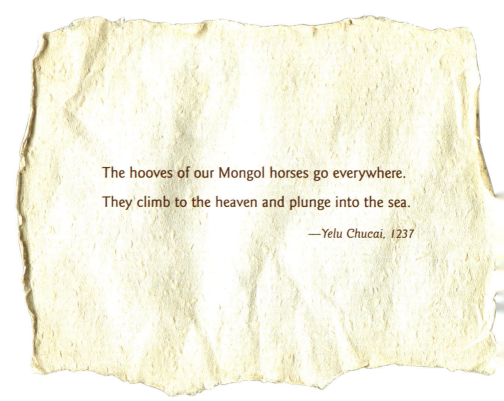

The hooves of our Mongol horses go everywhere.
They climb to the heaven and plunge into the sea.

—*Yelu Chucai, 1237*

Genghis Khan was gone. He had left his descendants a
great empire—and a great duty to protect and maintain
it. But first, his people had to formally choose his heir.
According to Kirakos Gandzaketsi (a thirteenth-century
Armenian writer), Genghis Khan had reflected on the
character of his remaining sons soon before he died.
"Chagatai is warlike and loves the army, but he is
arrogant; . . . Tolui is also a victorious warrior, but he is

mean; . . . Ogodei, however, has from childhood been gifted and generous."

At a kurultai in 1229, Ogodei became the Great Khan, in keeping with Genghis's wishes. And he did indeed prove himself generous—perhaps to a fault. Ogodei began his reign by declaring some lofty goals. *The Secret History* quotes him, saying, "Let all my subjects live in peace and happiness, with their feet on the ground; with their hands on the earth. . . . While I sit on this throne made by my father the Khan no one will go hungry for their daily broth."

But Ogodei's generosity spent much of the wealth his father had acquired. And he wasn't a great leader—he lacked the vision and talent of his father. Fortunately, he did have some skilled advisers, including Yelu Chucai, who had also counseled Genghis.

A new round of campaigns soon began, and this time Mongol forces set out in several directions simultaneously. The first and nearest target was, yet again, China. It was only in 1234—seven years after Genghis's death and following twenty more years of struggle there—that the Mongols finally defeated the Jin Empire. On the heels of this victory, they progressed southward to confront the Song dynasty.

Meanwhile, another force set out for Russia and Europe. Information gathered during Jebe and Subodei's great raid was used for later ventures into Kievan Rus, Volga Bulgaria, and further. In addition, Jochi's son Batu was already in that area. Because Jochi had died before Genghis, his share of his father's empire was divided among his sons Batu, Orda, and Shiban. They took over the Mongols' holdings around the Caucasus and in southern Russia. Batu would emerge as the strongest and most talented leader of the brothers, eventually founding his own realm. Known as the Kipchak Khanate, it was also called the Golden Horde.

Between the late 1230s and early 1240s, Batu launched successful campaigns into Russia, the future Ukraine, Poland, and Hungary. In late 1241, his troops were on the threshold of attacking Vienna, the capital of Austria. But then Ogodei Khan died, and Batu turned back to take part in the succession decision.

Batu's campaigns marked the farthest west that Mongol troops ever reached. But they by no means marked the end of the Mongol conquests. After a lengthy period of dispute, Ogodei's son Guyuk became the Great Khan in 1246 and planned to send troops deeper into eastern Europe. His time on the throne was extremely short lived, however, as he died in 1248 of illnesses related to severe alcoholism. Next in line came Tolui's son, Mongke, who ruled as Great Khan from 1251 to 1259. Under his reign, Mongol forces enjoyed successes against China's Song dynasty. They also made further incursions into Persia, taking the major city of Baghdad.

In 1260 Genghis's grandson Kublai became Great Khan. The second son of Tolui, he proved to be a more talented leader than his three predecessors. In addition to being the Mongol Empire's khan, in 1271 he founded the Yuan dynasty in China and became its first emperor. This new dynasty had its capital near modern-day Beijing. Once Mongol forces defeated the Song dynasty in 1279, the Yuan realm governed all of China.

It was at about this point that the Mongol Empire reached its largest. In addition to taking China, Kublai Khan's forces

This fourteenth-century Persian manuscript illumination shows Mongke Khan's attack on Baghdad.

invaded Japan in the 1270s and 1280s. They also struck Korea in 1270 (continuing a series of attacks that had begun in the 1230s), Myanmar in 1277 and the 1280s, Vietnam in the 1280s, and Java in 1292. While some of these expeditions succeeded at first, they largely failed to take new territory in the long term. Kublai Khan died in 1294.

CRACKS IN THE MONOLITH

Following Kublai Khan's death, the vast Mongol Empire split into four smaller realms. The Yuan dynasty continued to

The Mongol Invasions Scroll *tells the story of the Mongol attacks on Japan. It was painted by a Japanese scribe around 1293.*

dominate China, and the Golden Horde held power over the Caucasus, southern Russia, and much of Kazakhstan. In addition, the Chagatai Khanate—ruled by Chagatai's descendants—covered central Asia (primarily Kyrgyzstan, Tajikistan, much of Uzbekistan, and northern Pakistan). Finally, the Ilkhanate ruled Persia, including Iran, Afghanistan, western Pakistan, and most of Turkmenistan and Turkey.

Over time—and beginning even in Genghis's lifetime—the empire and its conquests had begun to change Mongol life and culture. For one thing, administering such a huge empire required some permanent outposts and the stationing of troops outside Mongolia. The vast amount of riches acquired in Genghis's conquests also had an impact. For years, goods and slaves had flowed out of conquered lands and into Mongolia. This bounty required a major change in

Mongol customs—the construction of permanent buildings to serve as warehouses. And Ogodei had built a palace and established a permanent capital named Karakorum. Yet another change occurred when Mongols in the Ilkhanate eventually began adopting Islam. They also shifted toward a more sedentary way of life, as did Mongol members of the Yuan dynasty. These changes may have hastened the empire's end. So did internal rivalries and arguments over succession, as well as outside challenges. Perhaps—covering more than 12 million square miles (31 million sq. km) at its height and claiming an estimated 100 million or more people as subjects—the empire had simply been stretched to the breaking point. In any case, by the end of the fourteenth century, Genghis Khan's former empire had collapsed under the combined weight of these challenges.

MAN OF MANY NAMES

He was born as Temujin. He lives on in history books as Genghis Khan.

Along with these names, the Mongol leader earned many other titles over the years. Some were glowing, while others showed how feared he was by enemies. They included Perfect Warrior, Master of Thrones and Crowns, Scourge of God, and the Accursed. After his death, his descendants also honored him with the title of Khagan, often translated as Great Khan or Khan of Khans.

RESTING IN PEACE, STILL

One of the greatest unsolved mysteries surrounding Genghis Khan is the location of his tomb. Since his death, rumors and tales about the khan's resting place have abounded. Many historians believe that it lies on Burkhan Khaldun or nearby. Mongol warriors and leaders were often buried at sites that held some special importance to them in life, so Genghis's sacred mountain would be the obvious choice. But they can only guess at exactly which mountain in Mongolia is the Burkhan Khaldun. Similarly, the Kentei Khan mentioned in Sagang Sechen's work is an entire range, not an individual peak.

This uncertainty doesn't mean people haven't searched, however. Many times over the years, people have believed—or simply claimed—that they have discovered the tomb. For example, a *New York Times* article from 1888 cited one man's claim that Genghis's body was "at a place called Kia-y-sen, in the land of the Ordos." The article went on to say that the khan's remains were "contained in a large silver coffin, which the Mongols will not show to strangers without some good reason. The coffin is wrapped round with rich stuffs, and numerous pilgrims come to kiss these and pay the same respect as they would to a living Emperor." Another article, in 1927, announced that a Russian archaeologist had found Genghis's tomb in the Gobi Desert. In the 1950s, the Chinese government built a mausoleum in southwestern Inner Mongolia, and though they admitted it held

In 2004, a team of Japanese and Mongolian archaeologists discovered artifacts that linked these thirteenth-century foundations to Genghis Khan's final years. However, research later suggested that this site was not the great leader's tomb.

no body, they began using the site as a place to pay respects to the leader. A U.S. and Mongolian group in 2001 claimed they'd found the real thing, and in 2004 Japanese and Mongolian archaeologists thought they had a lead east of modern Ulaanbaatar. But all of these discoveries have turned out to be false rumors or simply mistakes. The mystery remains.

LASTING LEGACY

To modern Mongolians, Genghis Khan is a hero—the father of the Mongol nation. Each year they hold celebrations in his honor. To the south, many Chinese people admire him for the legacy of his descendants' Yuan dynasty.

Observers in central Asia and the Middle East, on the other hand, have long viewed him and his Mongol forces as bloodthirsty and cruel. The conquests carried out by Genghis and his successors also struck terror into the hearts of Europeans, who saw the Mongols as barbarians.

Without a doubt, Genghis Khan and his forces were responsible for a vast number of deaths. Especially once his troops ventured into China and other lands outside the Mongolian steppes, they visited an increasing amount of suffering on their enemies. Stories of millions of innocent deaths spread quickly through the afflicted lands and beyond. These accounts were frequently told by the defeated people, and they may sometimes have exaggerated the atrocities that took place. But without question, Genghis Khan's campaigns left hundreds of thousands dead and wreaked a huge amount of destruction.

In recent times, however, some historians have urged those who study Genghis Khan to take a second look. They argue that the man and his deeds must be understood in context. In Mongol warfare—and that of much of the world at that time—life was fairly cheap. Success was of the greatest value. Genghis's troops used terror to achieve that success.

It is nevertheless impossible to ignore the many deaths that occurred at Genghis's command. It is equally impossible, however, to deny that Genghis was a talented leader and must also have been a charismatic man. Even as he struck the greatest fear into his enemies, he inspired the deepest devotion among his closest comrades. And he truly appears to have transformed his world in positive ways, as well. His empire brought a stability to the Mongol peoples and to central Asia that had never before existed. His unification of the Mongol tribes forged a new national identity among them that still exists in modern times. It is this accomplishment that gives him the title of father of Mongolia. His policy of religious tolerance is also noteworthy, as it was uncommon for the era. He changed nomadic governance by advancing the warrior meritocracy—a system rewarding individuals based on their actions and achievements, rather than by the accident of birth into a noble family. Beyond his homeland, his conquests vastly increased trade between East and West and, at the same time, opened corridors of communication and cultural exchange spanning huge distances and diverse peoples. Some historians credit him with creating a revolutionary Pax Mongolica (Mongol Peace), although other scholars see the title as a bit of an overstatement.

GENGHIS THE SIXTEEN MILLIONTH

In addition to his many other marks on the world, Genghis Khan also left behind a genetic legacy. Studies conducted in the early 2000s showed that Genghis may be a distant ancestor of as many as 16 million men living in modern Asia and Europe—or approximately one of every two hundred men in the world.

One domino-like theory even connects Genghis Khan's conquests to one of the world's magnificent time periods. The theory begins with a disaster. In the mid-1300s, the Mongols may have unleashed their most deadly weapon yet—although they probably had no intentions of doing so. Scholars believe that Mongol troops (as well as Muslim traders) carried the bubonic plague into western Asia. Major outbreaks of this fatal and highly infectious disease had earlier occurred in China. From western Asia, merchants carried them across the Mediterranean Sea to Europe, where historians estimate it took the lives of one- to two-thirds of the population. This catastrophic outbreak became known as the Black Death. In just five years, it killed an estimated 25 million people in Europe alone.

This staggering death toll changed the face of Europe for centuries. In its wake, devastated societies had to rebuild themselves—and most did not follow the former models. Massive social and economic upheaval took place, as peasant uprisings across the continent overthrew the old order.

In turn, these social changes may have sparked the Renaissance, a great cultural flowering in Europe that spanned the fourteenth through the seventeenth centuries. The Renaissance (the name literally means "rebirth") saw dramatic advancements in religion, philosophy, science, and other areas of human achievement. It produced artists such as Leonardo da Vinci and Michelangelo, authors such as Shakespeare and Dante, and scientists including Copernicus and Galileo.

Even if this theory is true, the relationship between Genghis Khan and the *Mona Lisa* is a distant one, at best.

But the very possibility of such a connection demonstrates his enduring effect on the world.

For all the back and forth, what emerges every time is something of an enigma. Persian historian Juzjani described Genghis Khan as "a man of tall stature, of vigorous build, robust in body, the hair on his face scanty and turned white, with cat's eyes, possessed of great energy, discernment, genius and understanding, awe-inspiring, a butcher, just, resolute, an overthrower of enemies, intrepid, sanguinary and cruel." Even in this account, written by a member of a people violently conquered by the Mongols, Genghis appears a complex and even confusing character.

And what about the future? Old Mongolian tales foretell the return of Genghis Khan as a great man who will once more lead his people back to prosperity and power. Renowned historian Owen Lattimore retells one of these legends. Genghis did not die, the story goes—he only "slept and from that sleep he has never wakened—but . . . he will awake and save his people."

PRIMARY SOURCE RESEARCH

To learn about historical events, people study many sources, such as books, websites, newspaper articles, photographs, and paintings. These sources can be separated into two general categories—primary sources and secondary sources.

A primary source is the record of an eyewitness. Primary sources provide firsthand accounts about a person or event. Examples include diaries, letters, autobiographies, speeches, newspapers, and oral history interviews. Libraries, archives, historical societies, and museums often have primary sources available on-site or on the Internet.

A secondary source is published information that was researched, collected, and written or otherwise created by someone who was not an eyewitness. These authors or artists use primary sources and other secondary sources in their research, but they interpret and arrange the source material in their own works. Secondary sources include history books, novels, biographies, movies, documentaries, and magazines. Libraries and museums are filled with secondary sources.

After finding primary and secondary sources, authors and historians must evaluate them. They may ask questions such as: Who created this document? What is this person's point of view? What biases might this person have? How trustworthy is this document? Just because a person was an eyewitness to an event does not mean that person recorded the whole truth about that event. For example, a soldier describing a battle might depict only the heroic actions of his unit and only the brutal behavior of the enemy. An account from a soldier on the opposing side might portray the same battle very differently. When sources disagree, researchers must decide through additional study which explanation makes the most sense. For this reason, historians consult a variety of primary and secondary sources. Then they can draw their own conclusions.

The Pivotal Moments in History series takes readers on a journey to important junctures in history that shaped our world as we know it today. Each event has been researched using both primary and secondary sources to enhance the awareness of the complexities of the materials and rich stories from which we draw our understanding of our shared history.

STUDYING GENGHIS KHAN

People who study and write about Genghis Khan and his conquests face a number of challenges. To begin with, most of Genghis's own people did not read or write at all during his lifetime. As a result, we have no journals kept by his soldiers or records written by Mongol officials. Even his great Yasa—the code of laws he ordered to be written—is lost. For modern scholars, the most important primary source is *The Secret History of the Mongols*, an account of Genghis's life and deeds. *The Secret History* also includes information about the reign of Ogodei Khan, Genghis's son and successor. An unknown author wrote this book in either 1228 or 1240. Although it does date from after Genghis's death, most scholars believe that the author was an official—probably fairly high ranking. This person was, after all, trusted with the important task of setting down the great khan's history, and as such, he was probably a well-regarded man who may well have known Genghis personally. Some scholars believe the author may even have been a family member.

Beyond *The Secret History*, we have only a few other primary sources to turn to. These, however, were written by non-Mongol peoples. In fact, most of these works are by enemies of the Mongols or by peoples defeated in the Mongol conquests. For example, Persian historian Ata-Malik Juvaini wrote *Tarikh-i Jahangushay*, or *History of the World Conqueror*, in the years following Genghis's death. This work focuses on the khan's conquests in central and western Asia. Another Persian author, Minhaj al-Siraj Juzjani, witnessed the Mongol attacks in central Asia and is believed to have glimpsed Genghis himself. In about 1260, he wrote *Tabaqat-i-Nasiri*, a history of the region that includes information about the Mongol conquests.

In addition to these works, we do have secondary sources to draw upon. The authors of these works used the records left by earlier writers. One of the most trusted and important is Persian historian Rashid al-Din's account of the Mongol conquests, *Collected Chronicles*. Rashid probably wrote this text between the late 1200s and early 1300s. He appears to have done careful research and to have drawn upon original Mongol sources that were later lost.

All of this writing and study over time gives us many resources on Genghis Khan. But with each level that we are further removed from the original sources, new room opens up for error, bias, and confusion to pollute the record. And when texts written in Chinese, Persian, or other languages are translated into English, this translation offers yet another opportunity for distortion and inaccuracy.

Even in Genghis's own time, some accounts of his deeds were probably unreliable. Sources—including the oldest ones we have—sometimes disagree on precise details of Genghis's life and conquests. And as tales of the Mongol conquests spread, they may very well have been exaggerated. Genghis Khan and his actions struck fear and anger into the hearts of people from China to Iran. As Juvaini and other Persian historians offered their accounts of the attacks on their homelands, they may not have been entirely objective. Some probably harbored deep resentment of these foreign conquerors, and this feeling may have influenced their writing. Others may have wished to please—or at least not to displease—their Mongol rulers.

For all of these reasons, each new author who chooses Genghis Khan as a subject has to make his or her own decisions about the most likely truth—although we will probably never know for certain. And no matter how hard writers try to make the best decisions they can, their choices inevitably reflect their own feelings and opinions. In the end, each reader must draw his or her own conclusions about an author's reliability and about the truth or falsehood of any given story.

Even when primary sources—or even reliable secondary sources—are in short supply, a variety of other tools can be helpful. For example, understanding what life and culture were like in Genghis's Mongol homeland may not tell us anything directly about the man himself, but they can shed some light on his character by revealing the influences that surrounded him. Similarly, information about the lands he conquered offers insight into how deeply his deeds changed the lives of Mongols, Chinese, Persians, and far beyond.

PRIMARY SOURCE: PORTRAITS

True primary sources about Genghis Khan's life are very rare. Rarer still are primary sources written by Mongols. Written works are not the only type of primary source, however. Paintings, sculpture, and other visual art can serve as helpful resources. But here, too, Genghis proves to be a bit of a mystery, as historians do not know of any portraits of him that were completed during his lifetime. Many paintings were later made by artists from Persia to Tibet, but these must be seen as secondary sources or even more distant.

The portraits that do exist can still be helpful and interesting to students of Genghis Khan, however. It is interesting to notice that many of these works do not match very well with the written descriptions of Genghis. Several authors around Genghis's time noted his reddish hair and green eyes. But most artwork shows him with dark hair and eyes.

This gap between written and visual representations shows how a person's preconceived ideas can influence his or her work. For example, no one knows exactly who the artist of the portrait on page 135 was or when it was created. But historians do know that the painter was Chinese. This portrait depicts the khan with dark eyes. His graying hair also looks as though it was once black rather than red. These features may give clues to how the Chinese artist's surroundings and influences affected his or her work. The painter may have simply showed Genghis in a way that was similar to the people among whom the artist lived.

This portrait of Genghis Khan was painted on stretched silk canvas by a Chinese artist. Art experts estimate that it was created sometime after 1279.

A lack of knowledge about a region or group of people can have an effect on sources too. An artist who lived far from Mongolia—perhaps one who has never seen a Mongol—might assume that they look very much like Chinese people because of Mongolia's geographic location near China. And personal biases or feelings can play a role as well. Just as conquered people might represent Genghis more bitterly in text than Mongol writers would, they might also draw or paint him to look menacing or cruel. When judging the value of a source, students and historians must take all of these factors into account.

TIMELINE

Note: Historians are unsure of many of the dates of specific events in Genghis's lifetime, and sources frequently disagree. Many of the dates that follow are therefore estimates, and some are based on Genghis's approximate date of birth being 1162, as used in this book.

1000S B.C.	Domesticated horses are a major part of Mongolian life.
500S B.C.	Siddhartha Gautama founds Buddhism in India.
CA. A.D. 386	Nestorius, the founder of Nestorian Christianity, is born.
600s	Muhammad founds Islam in Saudi Arabia.
960	China's Song dynasty is established.
1038	The Xi Xia kingdom is formed in the area that makes up modern Tibet.
1115	The Jin dynasty emerges in northern China.
1127	The Jin dynasty defeats the Song dynasty and pushes them into southern China.
1130s–1140s	Many Mongol groups fight the Jin.
1162	Genghis Khan is born as Temujin. His parents are Yesugei and Hoelun.

1171	Temujin meets Borte, his future wife. Yesugei dies, probably due to poisoning. Temujin and his family are abandoned by their clan.
MID-1170s	Temujin and his brother Kassar kill their half brother Begter.
1176	Taijut chieftain Targoutai Kiriltuk attacks Temujin's camp and captures him. Temujin is held prisoner before escaping with the help of Sorkhan Shira.
LATE 1170s	Temujin meets Jamuka, who later becomes his anda brother. Temujin's family suffers the theft of all but one of their horses. Temujin, with the help of a youth named Borchu, recovers the horses.
1178	Borte comes to live with Temujin as his wife. Temujin approaches Toghrul, and they form an alliance. Around this time, Temujin meets Jelme.
1181	Merkit raiders attack Temujin's camp. He finds shelter at Burkhan Khaldun, but the attackers seize Borte. Temujin, Toghrul, and Jamuka join forces and defeat the Merkits. After Borte's return, the couple's son Jochi is born.
1183	Jamuka and Temujin separate.
1184	Queen Tamar takes power in the kingdom of Georgia.

1190	Temujin's followers attend a kurultai and elevate him to the position of khan.
EARLY 1190s	Temujin and Jamuka meet in battle, and Temujin is defeated.
1195	Temujin (possibly with Toghrul's help) leads Mongol forces against the Tatars and is victorious. He gains still more supporters.
CA. 1200	Jamuka takes the title of Gurkhan. Temujin and Toghrul fight Jamuka's coalition forces. Jamuka flees, but Temujin and Toghrul wipe out Jamuka's Taijut allies. Temujin meets Jebe and accepts him as a follower.
1202	Temujin and Toghrul win a major victory over the Tatars.
1203	Temujin is defeated in a battle with Senggum and Toghrul's forces. He and a reduced number of followers retreat to Baljuna.
1204	Temujin defeats Toghrul and Senggum's forces. He goes on to defeat Naiman forces. Jamuka is eventually captured and executed.
1206	Temujin takes the title Genghis Khan.
EARLY 1200s	Genghis orders the writing of the Yasa.
1209	The Mongols confront Xi Xia forces.

1210	Genghis and the Xi Xia leader agree to a peace settlement.
1211	Genghis holds a kurultai to discuss plans for attacking the Jin dynasty's empire. Soon afterward, Mongol forces move south to attack Jin settlements in northern China. These battles begin a long cycle of war between Mongol and Jin forces.
CA. 1213	Genghis's brother Kassar dies in China.
1215	Genghis Khan places his general Muqali in charge of the ongoing Jin campaign.
CA. 1217	Genghis assigns his commander Jebe to fight Kuchlug and the Kara-Khitan realm. Jebe wins a relatively easy victory.
CA. 1219	A caravan of Muslim traders is killed at the decree of Khwarazm leaders. After attempts at peaceful reconciliation apparently fail, Genghis and thousands of troops march westward to fight the Khwarazm Empire. On the realm's eastern borders, he splits his forces into several groups.
1220	Mongol troops sack Bukhara. The Khwarazm shah, Muhammad, flees, and Genghis sends Jebe and Subodei after him. Meanwhile, troops led by Genghis's son Jochi begin a

siege of the city of Gurganj. Jochi's forces are joined by a group led by Ogodei and Chagatai, two of Genghis's other sons. Shah Muhammad dies.

1221   Jebe and Subodei begin the Great Raid through Armenia, the Caucuasus, and beyond. Forces led by Genghis's youngest son, Tolui, sack Nishapur (in modern-day Iran). Later that year, Shah Muhammad's son Jalal al-Din leads forces to a rare victory over Mongol troops near Kabul (in modern Afghanistan).

1222   Jebe and Subodei's troops defeat a coalition force of Kipchaks and Russians in a clash known as the Battle of the Kalka River. They later lose a battle to the Bulgars.

1223   The Mongol army begins heading homeward.

1225   Genghis and his soldiers return to Mongolia.

1226   A new campaign against Xi Xia takes place.

1227   Jochi dies (or possibly died in late 1226). In late summer, Genghis Khan dies.

1229   Ogodei becomes khan.

1234   Mongol forces defeat the Jin dynasty.

LATE 1230s   Jochi's son Batu leads campaigns in Russia,

the future Ukraine, and eastern Europe.

1241	Mongol forces reach their farthest point westward when Batu turns back from outside of Austria. Ogodei dies and Toregene, one of his wives, becomes regent for several years.
1246	Guyuk (Ogodei's son) becomes Great Khan.
1251	Tolui's son Mongke succeeds Guyuk as khan.
1260	Kublai (grandson of Genghis Khan) takes power.
1271	Kublai Khan founds China's Yuan dynasty.
1279	Mongol forces defeat the Song dynasty in southern China. The Mongol Empire reaches its largest point and stands as the largest connected empire the world had yet seen.
1294	Kublai Khan dies, and the empire fragments.
MID-1300s	The Black Death ravages the Middle East and Europe.
LATE 1300s	The Renaissance begins in Europe.
1962	The Mongolian government erects a monument in honor of the seven hundredth anniversary of Genghis Khan's birth.
1965	Omar Sharif stars as Temujin in a Hollywood movie called *Genghis Khan*.

1995	*Time* magazine names Genghis Khan as the "Man of the Millennium."
2004	Yet another excursion to find Genghis Khan's tomb ends without a discovery.
2007	Qi Zhongyi, the last Mongolian prince living in China, dies at the age of eighty-one.

GLOSSARY

AIRAG: fermented mare's milk. This staple of the Mongol diet is also called koumiss.

ANDA: the Mongol oath of blood brotherhood

ANIMISM: a religion having many deities that inhabit and represent facets of the natural world. The major deity in Mongol animism is Tenger Etseg, or Blue Heaven.

BUDDHISM: a religion founded by the monk Siddhartha Gautama (Buddha) in India in the 500s B.C. Buddhism gained widespread influence in China between the A.D. 300s and 500s.

CAVALRY: soldiers on horseback

CLAN: a family group

GER: a traditional Mongol home made of woolen cloth over a round wooden frame. Gers are also known as yurts.

ISLAM: a religion founded in seventh-century Saudi Arabia by the prophet Muhammad. In the 600s and 700s, Islam spread rapidly northward and westward in the region known in modern times as the Middle East.

KHAN: a Mongol chieftain or leader

KURULTAI: a traditional Mongol council or conference

NESTORIANISM: a branch of Christianity founded by Nestorius in the early A.D. 400s, in the region that later became Turkey. Nestorians believe that Jesus's human and divine selves were separate. The religion reached China and Mongolia by the 600s and 700s.

NOKHOR: a Mongol who voluntarily chooses to follow a chieftain who is not of his own clan

ORDU: a group of the same clan's gers, all set up in the same general area

SHAMAN: in Mongol spirituality, a figure who acted as a mediator for humans and the spirit world. Shamans were very important in Mongol communities.

VASSAL: a person, group, or realm that is subordinate to another

YASA: the code of laws that Genghis Khan ordered to be written

WHO'S WHO?

BATU (CA. 1205–1255) Son of Jochi and grandson of Genghis, Batu was a talented leader and military commander who became the first khan of the Golden Horde, ruling over parts of Russia and the Caucasus. The Golden Horde was also known as the Kipchak Khanate.

BORTE (CA. 1161–1224) Like Temujin's mother, Hoelun, Borte was a member of the Ongirad clan. She and Temujin were married when she was about seventeen years old. She remained his principal wife throughout her lifetime and was the mother of his four sons, as well as several daughters. She also appears to have been a trusted adviser and confidant of Genghis. While Genghis Khan usually took a wife with him on major campaigns, Borte generally stayed behind in Mongolia and appears to have had some role in managing the Mongol Empire from its heartland. Historians believe she died there several years before Genghis's own death, sometime between 1219 and 1224. Modern Mongolians regard Borte as a Grand Empress and a heroine.

CHAGATAI (CA. 1185–1242) Genghis and Borte's second son, Chagatai, had a role in creating his father's Yasa and also led several military campaigns. After Genghis's death, Chagatai was granted lands in central Asia as his realm, and his descendants formed what later became known as the Chagatai Khanate in this region.

JOCHI (CA. 1185–1227) The first son of Genghis Khan and Borte, Jochi grew up to be a skilled military commander. He led missions in the Khwarazm campaign, defeating and capturing many towns. However, because some doubt existed about whether he was Genghis's biological son (due to Borte's abduction by the Merkits), he was not chosen as his father's successor. After the Khwarazm wars ended, Jochi chose to stay behind in the lands granted to him in the western empire. He died several months before his father, in 1227 or possibly late 1226.

KUBLAI (1215–1294) Kublai was Genghis Khan's grandson (son of Tolui) and would prove to be the last of the Mongol Empire's great khans. Before becoming khan, he had been in charge of Chinese territory belonging to the Mongol Empire. In 1260, following the death of his brother Mongke, Kublai fought Ariq, another of his brothers, for control of the empire. This civil war lasted for about four years, finally ending in Kublai's victory. He also became the first emperor of China's Yuan dynasty in 1271. While he appears to have been a fairly good ruler, by the time of his death, the empire could no longer hold together.

SHAH ALA AL-DIN MUHAMMAD II (? –1221) Ala al-Din Muhammad II was born to a Persian leader named Takash (sometimes called Ala al-Din Tekish). In about 1200, following his father's death, Muhammad II took power of the Khwarazm lands. In the subsequent years, he succeeded in expanding his realm significantly. For example, in the span of about five years, he took over a significant amount of Persian territory from the Seljuk Turks, a powerful dynasty that then ruled much of western Asia. He also allied with Kuchlug to overthrow the Kara-Khitan realm's Gurkhan. Yet he also appears to have been an extremely incompetent ruler, who was much hated by his subjects. After making several grave tactical errors that brought Genghis's wrath unto his empire, Muhammad eventually fled the destruction of his realm. He eluded Jebe and Subodei long enough to die of an unknown illness (possibly pleurisy) on a small island in the Caspian Sea.

OGODEI (CA. 1186–1241) Ogodei was Genghis and Borte's third son. Before Genghis's campaign to Khwarazm, he and his sons agreed to name Ogodei as the great khan's heir. Ogodei took power at a kurultai in 1229 and took the title Khagan (Great Khan). Under his rule, Mongol forces defeated the Jin, began a campaign against the Song, and also drove farther into Russia and beyond. Ogodei was not as skilled a leader as his father, however, in part because he appears to have been a very heavy drinker. This habit seems to have prevented him from effectively governing at times, during which Toregene, one of his wives, apparently helped fulfill his duties. In any case, the empire remained strong and growing at his death, which appears to have been alcohol-related.

SUBODEI (CA. 1176–1248) Subodei was one of Genghis Khan's greatest generals. A member of a northern Mongol tribe, apparently one of the "forest peoples," he appears to have become one of Genghis's followers in the early 1200s. He was a loyal friend to Genghis. He also soon proved himself to be a brilliant military strategist. His success in battle earned him a place among Genghis's four "dogs of war," alongside Jebe, Jelme, and Jelme's brother Kublai. Together with Jebe, Subodei carried out the bold Great Raid. After Genghis's death, Subodei joined Batu and his forces in further campaigns in Russia and eastern Europe, and remained a warrior and commander into old age. After a final campaign in China, he died in Mongolia.

TOGHRUL (?–1203) Also known as Wang Khan or Ong Khan, Toghrul was a Kerait leader who became one of Genghis's allies and later one of his enemies. Toghrul had been the anda brother of Genghis's father, Yesugei, and when Genghis (then Temujin) was in his late teens, he approached the older and more powerful leader to form an alliance. When the two later came into conflict, Toghrul was captured and killed by Naiman warriors following a battle against the Mongols. Toghrul is sometimes associated with the figure of Prester John, an apparently mythological Christian king in Asia. Legends about Prester John abounded in Europe between the 1100s and 1600s, and John was probably based on a combination of many real historical leaders. As a Nestorian ruler, Toghrul may well have been one of these leaders.

TOLUI (CA. 1190–1232) Tolui was Genghis Khan's fourth and youngest son with Borte. According to Mongolian custom, this position as youngest made him the "keeper of the hearth," or the protector of the family's homeland. In keeping with this idea, Tolui's realm after his father's death was the Mongolian heartland. After Genghis's death, many high-ranking Mongol leaders favored Tolui over Ogodei as successor—possibly because Tolui had proven to be a more skillful military commander—but Tolui declined the position and followed Genghis's wishes to place Ogodei in power. Tolui went on to have four powerful sons with his wife Sorghaghtani Beki (a niece of Kerait leader Toghrul). The oldest, Mongke, was the fourth great khan of the Mongol Empire, while their third son, Hulagu, was a khan in the Ilkhanate realm in Persia. Their youngest son, Ariq, attempted to become khan after Mongke's death but was defeated by his brother Kublai, Tolui and Sorghaghtani's second son and the last great khan of the Mongol Empire.

SOURCE NOTES

4 Paul Kahn, *The Secret History of the Mongols: The Origin of Chingis Khan* (Boston: Cheng and Tsui Company, 1998), 7.

5 Ibid., 32.

16 David Morgan, *The Mongols* (Malden, MA: Blackwell Publishing, 1990), 37.

20 Ibid., 85.

20 Ibid.

24 Kahn, *The Secret History*, 13.

25 Ibid., 12.

27 Ibid., 13.

28 Ibid., 15.

29 Ibid., 19.

34 Ibid., 27.

35 Ibid., 29.

38 Ibid., 37.

38 Ibid., 41.

40 Ibid., 114.

43 Ibid., 44–45.

45 Paul Ratchnevsky, *Genghis Khan: His Life and Legacy* (Malden, MA: Blackwell Publishing, 1992), 41.

46 Ibid., 50.

51 Ibid., 73.

52 John Man, *Genghis Khan: Life, Death, and Resurrection* (New York: St. Martin's Press, 2004), 97.

54 Kahn, *The Secret History*, 98.

55 Ibid., 110.

58 Kahn, *The Secret History*, 116.

59 Ibid., 117–118.

61 Leo De Hartog, *Genghis Khan: Conqueror of the World* (New York: Tauris Parke Paperbacks, 2006), 42.

68 Ibid., 116.

68 Ibid.

72 Kahn, *The Secret History*, 146.

76 Ratchnevsky, *Genghis Khan: His Life and Legacy*, 104.

78 Ibid.

79 Kahn, *The Secret History*, 149.

82 Ratchnevsky, *Genghis Khan: His Life and Legacy*, 109.

82 Ratchnevsky, *Genghis Khan: His Life and Legacy*, 145.

87 Kahn, *The Secret History*, 148.

90 Man, *Genghis Khan: Life, Death, and Resurrection*, 153.

96 Ratchnevsky, *Genghis Khan: His Life and Legacy*, 123.

96 Kahn, *The Secret History*, 152.

97 Ibid.

97 Ibid.

98 Ibid., 155.

98 Ibid., 157.

102 Man, *Genghis Khan: Life, Death, and Resurrection*, 171.

115 Ibid., 240.

116 Kahn, *The Secret History*, 165.

117 Ibid., 190.

118 Jack Weatherford, *Genghis Khan and the Making of the Modern World* (New York: Three Rivers Press, 2004), 81.

118 Ratchnevsky, *Genghis Khan: His Life and Legacy*, 128.

129 J. J. Saunders, *The History of the Mongol Conquests* (Philadelphia: University of Pennsylvania Press, 1971), 63.

129 Man, *Genghis Khan: Life, Death, and Resurrection*, 247–248.

123 Harold Lamb, *Genghis Khan: Emperor of All Men* (New York: Bantam Books, 1965), 1.

123 Ibid.,10.

123 De Hartog, *Conqueror of the World*, 132.

124 *New York Times*, "The Grave of Genghis Khan," November 5, 1888.

124 Ibid.

SELECTED BIBLIOGRAPHY

PRIMARY AND SECONDARY SOURCES

Kahn, Paul. *The Secret History of the Mongols: The Origin of Chingis Khan.* Boston: Cheng and Tsui Company, 1998.

Onon, Urgunge. *The Secret History of the Mongols: The Life and Times of Chinggis Khan.* Richmond, U.K.: Curzon Press, 2001.

OTHER SOURCES

Chua-Eoan, Howard. "Genghis Khan." *Time.* December 31, 1999. http://www.time.com/time/magazine/article/0,9171,993031,00.html (July 16, 2007).

Curtin, Jeremiah. *The Mongols: A History.* Cambridge, MA: Da Capo Press, 2003. (First published in 1908 by Little, Brown and Company).

De Hartog, Leo. *Genghis Khan: Conqueror of the World.* New York: Tauris Parke Paperbacks, 2006.

Encyclopedia Britannica. *Encyclopedia Britannica online.* 2007. http://www.britannica.com (July 16, 2007).

Lamb, Harold. *Genghis Khan: Emperor of All Men.* New York: Bantam Books, 1965. (First published in 1927 by Garden City Publishing).

Man, John. *Genghis Khan: Life, Death, and Resurrection.* New York: St. Martin's Press, 2004.

Morgan, David. *The Mongols.* Malden, MA: Blackwell Publishing, 1990.

National Geographic Society. *National Geographic.* 2007. http://www.nationalgeographic.com (July 16, 2007).

New York Times Company. *The New York Times on the Web.* 2007. http://www.nytimes.com (July 16, 2007).

Polo, Marco, and Rustichello of Pisa. "The Travels of Marco Polo: Volume 1." *Project Gutenberg.* January 8, 2004. http://www.gutenberg.org/etext/10636 (September 13, 2007).

———. "The Travels of Marco Polo: Volume 2." *Project Gutenberg.* May 22, 2004. http://www.gutenberg.org/etext/12410 (September 13, 2007).

Ratchnevsky, Paul. *Genghis Khan: His Life and Legacy*. Malden, MA: Blackwell Publishing, 1992.

Rossabi, Morris. "All the Khan's Horses." *Columbia University: Asian Topics in World History: The Mongols in World History*. 2004. http://afe.easia.columbia.edu/mongols (July 16, 2007).

Saunders, J. J. *The History of the Mongol Conquests*. Philadelphia: University of Pennsylvania Press, 1971.

Waley, Arthur. "Notes on the 'Yüan-ch'ao pi-shih.'" *Bulletin of the School of Oriental and African Studies, University of London* 23, no. 3 (1960): 523–529.

Weatherford, Jack. *Genghis Khan and the Making of the Modern World*. New York: Three Rivers Press, 2004.

FURTHER READING AND WEBSITES

BOOKS

Behnke, Alison. *China in Pictures*. Minneapolis: Twenty-First Century Books, 2003.

Childress, Diana. *Marco Polo's Journey to China*. Minneapolis: Twenty-First Century Books, 2008.

DuTemple, Lesley. *The Great Wall of China*. Minneapolis: Twenty-First Century Books, 2003.

Hanson, Jennifer L. *Mongolia*. New York: Facts On File, 2004.

Kort, Michael G. *The Handbook of East Asia*. Minneapolis: Twenty-First Century Books, 2006.

McNeese, Tim. *Marco Polo and the Realm of Kublai Khan*. Philadelphia: Chelsea House Publishers, 2006.

Nicolle, David. *Kalka River, 1223: Genghiz Khan's Mongols Invade Russia*. Westport, CT: Praeger, 2005.

Sanders, Alan J. K. *Mongolian Phrasebook*. Oakland: Lonely Planet Publications, 1995.

153

Woods, Michael, and Mary B. Woods. *Ancient Warfare*. Minneapolis: Twenty-First Century Books, 2000.

WEBSITES AND FILMS

Country Profile: Mongolia
http://news.bbc.co.uk/2/hi/asia-pacific/country_profiles/1235560.stm
In addition to this overview of modern Mongolia, the BBC offers news and updates on current events in and involving the nation.

In Our Time: Genghis Khan
http://www.bbc.co.uk/radio4/history/inourtime/inourtime_20070201
.shtml
Listen to a radio program from the BBC discussing Genghis Khan and his deeds, especially as a military commander and the founder of a vast empire.

The Land of Genghis Khan
http://www.nationalgeographic.com/genghis
This *National Geographic* site explores modern Mongolia, the Mongol conquests, the life of Genghis himself, and other topics related to the great khan.

Modern Mongolia: Reclaiming Genghis Khan
http://www.museum.upenn.edu/Mongolia/index.shtml#
This website is a joint project by the University of Pennsylvania's Museum of Archaeology and Anthropology and the National Museum of Mongolian History in Mongolia. It presents an online museum of historical and modern Mongolia, information about Genghis, and a discussion of his relevance in modern times.

Mongolian Crossing
http://www.nationalgeographic.com/ngm/0310/feature5/index.html
Another *National Geographic* site offers information on modern nomadic life in Mongolia. Be sure to click on the photographs for vivid images of the Mongolian landscape, people, and lifestyle.

The Mongols in World History
http://afe.easia.columbia.edu/mongols
This website from Columbia University provides information on the

Mongol conquests, major Mongol leaders (including Genghis Khan), and Mongol lifestyles in Genghis's time.

The Story of the Weeping Camel. DVD. Washington, D.C.: National Geographic World Films, 2004.
This documentary-style movie follows a modern nomadic Mongolian family and shows many aspects of their daily life.

The Story of the Weeping Camel
http://www.nationalgeographic.com/weepingcamel/
The companion website to the documentary film provides background information on Mongolian life, Mongolian camels, and more—along with vivid, full-color photographs.

Wild Horses of Mongolia
http://www.pbs.org/wnet/nature/mongolia
Learn more about the history of Mongolian horses and their place in modern Mongolian life. Be sure to click on video links at this PBS site to see the animals in action.

INDEX

ABOUT THE AUTHOR

Alison Behnke is an author and editor of books for young readers. Her other books include *China in Pictures*, *The Conquests of Alexander the Great*, and *Afghanistan in Pictures*. She loves to read, write, and travel, and she lives in Rome, Italy.

PHOTO ACKNOWLEDGMENTS

The images in this book were used with the permission of: © AAAC/ Topham/The Image Works, p. 6; © Laura Westlund/Independent Picture Service, pp. 8, 92, 101, 113; © Bildarchiv Preussischer Kulturbesitz/ Art Resource, NY, pp. 9, 68; © age fotostock/SuperStock, p. 13; © Persian School/The Bridgeman Art Library/Getty Images, p. 23; © The Bridgeman Art Library/SuperStock, p. 30; © SuperStock, Inc./SuperStock, pp. 37, 56; © Burstein Collection/CORBIS, p. 50; © Visual Arts Library (London)/ Alamy, pp. 54, 121; The Granger Collection, New York, p. 62; © MPI/ Hulton Archive/Getty Images, p. 75; © Werner Forman/Topham/The Image Works, p. 86; The Art Archive/Bibliothèque Nationale Paris, p. 88; © HIP/ The Image Works, p. 98; The Art Archive/British Library, p. 103; © Robert Harding Picture Library Ltd/Alamy, p. 107; © Mary Evans Picture Library/ Alamy, p. 111; © The British Library/HIP/The Image Works, p. 116; The Art Archive/Laurie Platt Winfrey, p. 122; AP Photo/The Japan-Mongol Joint Research Team, HO, p. 125; AP Photo/National Palace Museum, HO, p. 135.

Front Cover: © Visual Arts Library (London)/Alamy.